Conquering Fourth Grade

Reading
Mathematics
Science
Social Studies
Writing

Jennifer Prior, Ph.D.

Publishing Credits

Corinne Burton, M.A.Ed., *President*; Conni Medina, M.A.Ed., *Managing Editor*; Emily R. Smith, M.A.Ed., *Content Director*; Lynette Ordoñez, *Editor*; Evan Ferrell, *Graphic Designer*; Lubabah Memon, *Assistant Editor*

Image Credits

pp. 8, 28, 43 Illustrations by Timothy J. Bradley; all other images from iStock and/or Shutterstock.

Standards

Shell Education
A division of Teacher Created Materials
5301 Oceanus Drive
Huntington Beach, CA 92649-1030
www.tcmpub.com/shell-education
ISBN 978-1-4258-1623-0

Table of Contents

Introduction
- Family Letter 4
- Suggested Family Activities. 5

Unit 1
- Language Arts 7–12
- Mathematics 13–16
- Social Studies 17
- Science. 18
- Critical Thinking. 19
- Game 20
- Extension Activities 21

Unit 2
- Language Arts 22–27
- Mathematics 28–31
- Social Studies 32
- Science. 33
- Critical Thinking. 34
- Game 35
- Extension Activities 36

Unit 3
- Language Arts 37–42
- Mathematics 43–46
- Social Studies 47
- Science. 48
- Critical Thinking. 49
- Game 50
- Extension Activities 51

Unit 4
- Language Arts 52–57
- Mathematics 58–61
- Social Studies 62
- Science. 63
- Critical Thinking. 64
- Game 65
- Extension Activities 66

Unit 5
- Language Arts 67–72
- Mathematics 73–76
- Social Studies 77
- Science. 78
- Critical Thinking. 79
- Game 80
- Extension Activities 81

Unit 6
- Language Arts 82–87
- Mathematics 88–91
- Social Studies 92
- Science. 93
- Critical Thinking. 94
- Game 95
- Extension Activities 96

Unit 7
- Language Arts 97–102
- Mathematics 103–106
- Social Studies 107
- Science. 108
- Critical Thinking. 109
- Game 110
- Extension Activities 111

Unit 8
- Language Arts 112–117
- Mathematics 118–121
- Social Studies 122
- Science. 123
- Critical Thinking. 124
- Game 125
- Extension Activities 126

Unit 9
- Language Arts 127–132
- Mathematics 133–136
- Social Studies 137
- Science. 138
- Critical Thinking. 139
- Game 140
- Extension Activities 141

Unit 10
- Language Arts 142–147
- Mathematics 148–151
- Social Studies 152
- Science. 153
- Critical Thinking. 154
- Game 155
- Extension Activities 156

Appendix
- Answer Key 157
- Skills and Standards in This Book . . . 165
- Certificate of Achievement 168

Dear Family,

Welcome to *Conquering Fourth Grade*. Fourth grade will be an exciting and challenging year for your child. This book is designed to supplement the concepts your child is learning in fourth grade and to strengthen the connection between home and school. The activities in this book are based on today's standards and provide practice in reading, word study, language, writing, mathematics, social studies, and science. It also features fun, yet challenging, critical-thinking activities and games. In addition to the activity sheets in this book, the end of each section also provides engaging extension activities.

Your child should complete one unit per month, including the extension activities. This will allow your child to think about grade-level concepts over a longer period of time. This also ensures that the book can be completed in one school year.

Keep these tips in mind as you work with your child this year:

- Set aside specific times each week to work on the activities.
- Have your child complete one or two activities each time, rather than an entire unit at one time.
- Keep all practice sessions with your child positive and constructive. If the mood becomes tense or you and your child get frustrated, set the book aside and find another time to practice.
- Help your child with instructions, if necessary. If your child is having difficulty understanding what to do, work through some of the problems together.
- Encourage your child to do his or her best work, and compliment the effort that goes into learning.

Enjoy the time learning with your child during fourth grade. Summer will be here before you know it!

Sincerely,

The Shell Education Staff

Suggested Family Activities

You can extend your child's learning by taking fun family field trips. A wide variety of experiences helps expand and develop a child's vocabulary. Field trips also provide greater context and meaning to his or her learning in school.

A Trip to a Zoo

Before your trip, create a scavenger hunt with a list of questions about different animals. Ask specific questions about each animal that your child is to find. Try to incorporate questions about the animal's habitat, lifestyles, eating habits, and so on. For example, *Find the smallest bird at the zoo. What kind of bird is it? What is its natural habitat?*

A Trip to a Library

Ask your child about a new skill he or she is interested in learning for the first time. Your child can then use the digital catalog to search for books on that skill. He or she can choose two books about the topic, check them out, and enjoy learning!

A Trip to a National Park

The National Park Service has a great program called Junior Rangers. If you go to a local park, check in with the rangers at the visitors center to see what tasks your child can complete to earn a Junior Ranger patch and/or certificate. Your child can also go to the WebRangers site (www.nps.gov/webrangers/) and check out a vacation spot, play games, and earn virtual rewards!

A Trip to a Museum

Pick an area of the museum, and have your child select an artifact or a piece of art without telling the rest of the family what it is. The family then tries to guess what the secret item is. Ask for clues that require a yes or no answer. For example, *Does the item have sharp teeth?* or *Is the item made out of clay?* The person who guesses the secret item correctly gets to choose the item in the next room.

A Trip to a Farmers' Market

Farmers' markets are great places to learn how different fruits and vegetables are grown. For each fruit or vegetable stand, have your child identify whether it is grown in the ground or on a bush or tree. Encourage your child to ask the seller/farmer about the steps it takes to grow the plant(s). Have your child pick out a new fruit or vegetable to buy and enjoy with dinner that night!

Suggested Family Activities *(cont.)*

By discussing the activities in this book, you can enhance your child's learning. But it doesn't have to stop there. The suggestions below provide even more ideas on how to support your child's education.

General Skills

- Make sure your child gets plenty of exercise. Children need about 60 minutes of physical activity each day. You may want to have your child sign up for a sport. Or you can do fun things as a family, such as swimming, riding bicycles, or hiking.
- Help your child become organized and responsible. Have places for your child to keep important things. Take time to set up a schedule together. Use a timer to keep track of time spent on different activities.

Reading Skills

- Set a reading time for the entire family at least once every other day. You can read aloud or read silently. Help your child choose books that are at comfortable reading levels and that are interesting to him or her.
- After reading, ask your child to summarize what he or she has just read.
- Read books to your child that are above his or her reading level. This allows your child to experience more complex vocabulary, sentences, and ideas.

Writing Skills

- Set up a writing spot for your child. Have all of his or her writing materials in one special place. Having a designated area to write will help your child see writing as an important activity.
- Encourage your child to keep a daily journal or diary. Have him or her spend 10 minutes a day writing an entry about the day, feelings, things to remember, likes and dislikes, and so on.

Mathematics Skills

- Use fun foods that are easy to divide to practice fractions. Ask questions such as, *If there are 16 slices of pizza and together we eat 4 slices, what fraction of the pizza did we eat?*
- Have your child estimate measurements while out in the community. For example: *This menu is about 8 inches wide. About how wide do you think the table is?*

Directions: Read the text, and answer the questions.

Amazing Manatees

Manatees are large mammals. They live in shallow bodies of water. They are migratory animals. They spend winters in Florida's rivers. In the summer, they move northwest. They have been sighted as far north as Massachusetts! Manatees are gentle herbivores. They eat grass and plants. Manatees can grow to be very large. Adults are about ten feet long. They weigh 800–1,200 pounds (363–544 kg). That's about the size of a small bus! Manatees are mammals, so they breathe air. They come up to the surface of the water when they need more air. Manatees can hold their breath for fifteen minutes!

1. What do manatees eat?
   - (A) fish
   - (B) plants
   - (C) snakes
   - (D) sharks

2. Which alternate title best fits the text?
   - (A) "The World of Mammals"
   - (B) "Riding on a Mini-Bus"
   - (C) "Living in Florida"
   - (D) "Manatees: Gentle Giants"

3. Which word has the same root as *migratory*?
   - (A) migraine
   - (B) migrate
   - (C) great
   - (D) grate

4. Migratory animals are animals that
   - (A) move from one place to another.
   - (B) eat other animals.
   - (C) stay in one place all year long.
   - (D) lay eggs.

5. What type of text would have a similar tone?
   - (A) a history book
   - (B) a science-fiction novel
   - (C) a science textbook
   - (D) a travel magazine

Reading

Reading

Directions: Read the text, and answer the questions.

The Worst Day Ever

It was the worst day ever! First, Melissa stepped in a puddle and got muddy water on her new jeans. Then, when she arrived at school, she couldn't find her homework. Melissa decided to tell her teacher what happened. She nervously went into the classroom.

"Mr. Harper, I'm sorry, but I forgot to bring my homework today."

Mr. Harper looked up from his papers. "Did you do the homework?"

"Yes, I did. I even put it in my folder, but I left my folder at home."

"Don't worry. The homework isn't due until tomorrow," said Mr. Harper.

What a relief! At least something went right.

1. What is this text about?
   - (A) winning a big prize
   - (B) a bad day
   - (C) doing homework
   - (D) planets and stars

2. Which alternative title best fits the text?
   - (A) "A Muddy Day"
   - (B) "Forgetting Homework"
   - (C) "Mr. Harper's Class"
   - (D) "A Terrible Day"

3. Which word indicates Melissa's feelings at the end of the text?
   - (A) relief
   - (B) least
   - (C) tomorrow
   - (D) worry

4. *It was the worst day ever!* is an example of
   - (A) a metaphor.
   - (B) hyperbole.
   - (C) personification.
   - (D) onomatopoeia.

Directions: The letters *c* and *g* make both soft (/s/ and /j/) and hard (/k/ and /g/) sounds. When a *c* or *g* is followed by *e*, *i*, or *y*, it usually makes the soft sound. When a *c* or *g* is followed by *a*, *o*, or *u*, it usually makes the hard sound. Write each word from the Word Bank in the correct column. Then, write two sentences that each use at least two words from the Word Bank.

Word Bank

- complete
- country
- bounce
- gentle
- magic
- voice
- copy
- germ
- guess
- gypsy

Soft Sound	Hard Sound

1. ______________________________

2. ______________________________

Language

Directions: Circle the words that should be capitalized in each sentence.

1. the spacecraft took eleven months to get to mars.
2. boothill graveyard is in tombstone, arizona.
3. the boston post road began as trails before the colonists came.
4. beijing used to be called peking.
5. "can we go there today?" mina's brother asked.
6. let's go to the store on main street.
7. lyla and ethan had a snack by sand hill river.
8. cole said, "maybe my dad can pick us up."
9. there are many lighthouses in the state of maine.
10. john and mary went to see their dad in the hospital.

Directions: Read the topics for an informative/explanatory paragraph on the Chihuahua, a breed of dog. Choose one topic, and put a check mark by it. Then, read the facts. Put stars by the facts that support the topic you choose.

Topics

_____ physical characteristics

_____ breed history

_____ temperament and personality

Facts

____ smallest breed of dog weighing 4 to 6 pounds

____ clay pots with dogs resembling modern Chihuahuas were found in Mexico in the year 100

____ can be long- or short-haired

____ considered a difficult breed to housebreak, or train

____ named after a state in Mexico called Chihuahua

____ intelligent and loyal to its owner

____ life expectancy of 12 to 20 years

____ possibly descended from the Fennec fox, which is small with big eyes and ears

____ coats can be any color, either solid or multicolored

____ like to burrow in pillows and blankets

Writing

Directions: Write an informative/explanatory paragraph about Chihuahuas. Include specific facts about the breed, such as their physical characteristics, breed history, or personality. Use the notes from page 11 to help you.

Remember!

A strong informative/explanatory paragraph should include:

- an introductory and a concluding sentence
- details that support the main idea

Directions: Solve each problem.

1. Lou's mass is 5 kg less than Don, who has a mass of 34 kg. What is Lou's mass?

   ____

2. Beverly has 130 pennies, which she has divided into stacks of 5. How many stacks does she have?

   ____

3. Bananas cost 19¢ each. How much will 5 bananas cost?

   ____

4. Three sisters are each making themselves one beaded necklace. They use 125 beads on each necklace. How many beads do they need?

   ____

5. It takes 5 bottles of water to fill a 20-liter tank. How many liters are in each bottle?

   ____

6. It takes David 15 minutes to ride his bike around the block. How many times can he ride around the block in 45 minutes?

   ____

7. If one ticket costs $3.00, how much do 13 tickets cost?

   ____

8. Our product is 72. The difference between us is 1. What numbers are we?

   ____

Mathematics

Mathematics

Directions: Solve each problem.

1. $26 - 9 =$ ________

2. $32 \div 4 =$ ________

3. $63 \div 9 =$ ________

4. 12 shared equally by 6 is ________.

5. $6 \times \square = 24$

6. $56 \div 8 =$ ________

7. $6 \times 9 =$ ________

8. $28 \div 4 =$ ________

Directions: Read the problem, and answer the questions.

A scientist estimates that there are three hundred five thousand, sixty-one fish in a lake. How do you write this number in standard form and expanded form?

1. How many digits are in the number when written in standard form? How do you know?

____

____

____

2. What are the values of the digits 3 and 6 in the problem?

____

____

3. In standard form, which place values have zeros?

____

____

4. Write three hundred five thousand, sixty-one in standard and in expanded form.

____

____

Problem Solving

Directions: Read and solve each problem.

Problem 1

A scientist estimates that there are two hundred ten thousand, one hundred one fish in a lake. How do you write this number in standard form and in expanded form?

List What You Know	Write Your Plan
Solve the Problem	**Look Back and Explain**

Problem 2

The scientist estimates there are 709,205 living species in the lake, including the fish. How do you write this number in expanded form and in word form?

List What You Know	Write Your Plan
Solve the Problem	**Look Back and Explain**

Directions: Answer the questions.

1. Who are the people in your family who make and enforce rules?

2. Who are the people in your community who make and enforce rules?

3. Why do they do this?

4. How do laws help people live peacefully together?

Science

Directions: Follow the steps in this experiment to discover how many reflections there are.

What You Need

- two flat mirrors
- protractor
- modeling clay
- clear tape
- object

What to Do

1. Use tape to hinge the two mirrors together. Use a protractor to set them at a 90° angle.

2. Place an object in front of the two mirrors.

   How many images do you see? ______________________

3. Reduce the angle to 60°, then 45°, then 30°. What do you see?

   60° ______________________

   45° ______________________

   30° ______________________

4. Describe the relationship between the angle and the number of images.

   ____

   ____

5. Separate the two mirrors, and place them parallel and facing each other. Use modeling clay to hold them in place.

6. Place the object between the two mirrors. Look into one mirror from slightly above or to one side.

   How many images do you see? ______________________

Directions: Every mini-grid must have one each of the letters A–F. Every column must have one each of the letters A–F. Every row must have one each of the letters A–F.

A			F		E
E		B			A
	A		C	F	
C	D				B
		A	E		
	E	C		A	

Directions: Play with a partner. Place a small paper clip in the center of the first circle. Place the point of a pencil through the paper clip to form a spinner. For each turn, use the pencil and paper clip to spin all three spinners. Write the number you create. After each player has had five turns, add up your scores. The person with the highest score wins.

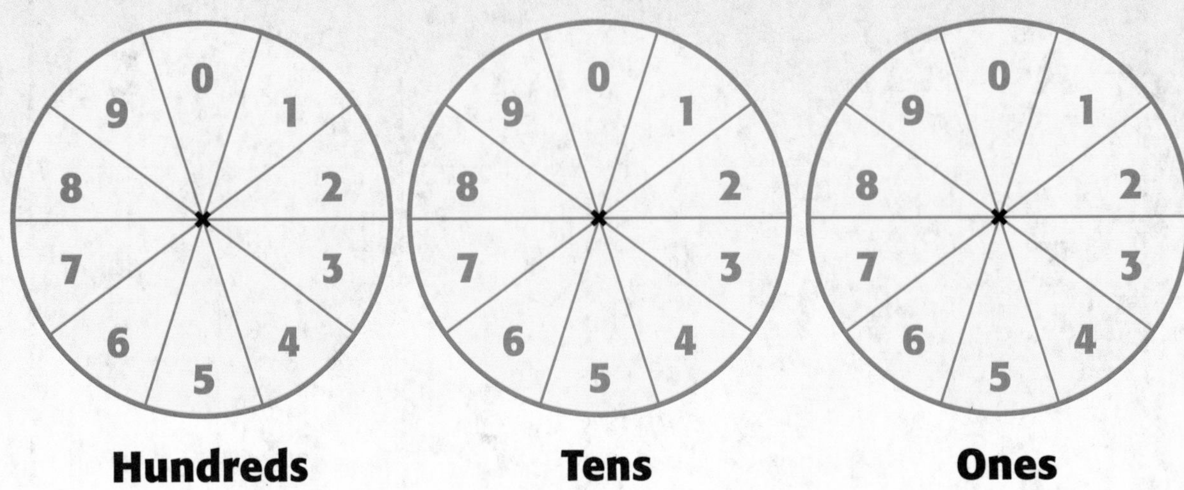

Player 1	Player 2
Total:	**Total:**

Spelling Activity

Write each word from the Word Bank on page 9 in your best cursive handwriting. After the letter *c* or *g*, trace the vowel in a colored pencil or marker.

Writing Activity

Reread your paragraph on page 12, checking for correct capitalization of proper nouns (including the name of the dog breed). Edit your paragraph as needed.

Mathematics Activity

Choose one of the problems from page 14, and write a word problem for it.

Science Activity

Draw a diagram of the mirrors and the object from the experiment on page 18. Draw a line showing how the object is reflected from the mirrors to your eyes.

Critical-Thinking Activity

Create your own sudoku puzzle. Start with a completed puzzle. Then, remove some letters. Test your puzzle to see if it can be solved with the letters you left.

Listening-and-Speaking Activity

Talk to your family about the rules at home. Ask them which rules they think are most important and why.

Reading

Directions: Read the text, and answer the questions.

Fire Safety

Fires can be dangerous, which is why fire safety is important. Here are some things you can do to keep your home safe:

- Always cook with an adult.
- Don't play in the kitchen.
- Keep towels and flammables away from the stove and heaters.
- Never place clothes or flammables on a lamp.
- Don't plug too many items into an outlet.
- Never play with matches or lighters.

1. What does the first sentence tell the reader about the text?
   - (A) This is about the best ways to start fires.
   - (B) This is about how to heat things without using fire.
   - (C) This is about tragedies that occurred because of fires.
   - (D) This is about how to be safe and prevent fires.

2. The word *flammables* has
   - (A) one syllable.
   - (B) two syllables.
   - (C) three syllables.
   - (D) none of the above

3. An antonym of *always* is
   - (A) never.
   - (B) don't.
   - (C) away.
   - (D) from.

4. What is the author's purpose?
   - (A) to instruct
   - (B) to scare
   - (C) to entertain
   - (D) to persuade

5. What is the main idea?
   - (A) Adults should do the cooking.
   - (B) Do not play with fire.
   - (C) You can prevent fires.
   - (D) Fires are very dangerous.

Reading

Directions: Read the text, and answer the questions.

A Brilliant Idea

Autumn was definitely here. The days were getting shorter, the air was cooler, and the leaves were falling from the trees. I was staring out my bedroom window one afternoon, watching the leaves tumbling across our lawn, when I got an idea. I raced downstairs.

"Mom," I called into the den. "I know how I can earn enough money to buy those sneakers we saw at the mall!"

Mom looked up from her computer. "And how's that, Leila?"

"People want their yards clean and tidy. I can rake up leaves for our neighbors."

A smile slowly spread across Mom's face. "Now that's a good idea!"

1. The dialogue in the text shows that Leila
   - (A) cannot rake leaves this autumn.
   - (B) is disappointed that her mother won't give her money.
   - (C) is excited about earning money.
   - (D) does not like autumn.

2. What is the root word in *tumbling*?
   - (A) tumble
   - (B) tremble
   - (C) trouble
   - (D) topple

3. Which strategy would help a reader define *definitely*?
   - (A) Read the text's last sentence.
   - (B) Say the word aloud.
   - (C) Write out the word.
   - (D) Find the word in a dictionary.

4. Which phrase from the text is an example of alliteration?
   - (A) I raced downstairs.
   - (B) I can rake up leaves
   - (C) watching the leaves
   - (D) a smile slowly spread

Spelling

Directions: When a word contains the letters *ou* together, the combination can make the /ow/ sound or the /aw/ sound. List the words in the chart according to the sounds they make. Then, write two sentences that each use at least one word from the Word Bank.

Word Bank

- mound
- sought
- ground
- surround
- bought
- brought
- hound
- thought
- astound
- fought

/ow/	/aw/

1. ____

____

____

____

____

2. ____

____

____

____

____

Directions: Write the missing punctuation in each sentence.

1. Owen said, "I'm getting tired. I think it's time to go home
2. Shall we pick up a pizza for dinner tonight " Riku's dad asked.
3. "What shall we do tomorrow " Kala asked.
4. I would like to travel on a train a ship, or a plane
5. "Stop, thief " cried the giant to Jack.
6. Amin likes to read books about writers
7. A famous ocean liner sank on April 15 1912.
8. The first snowboard was invented in Muskegon Michigan.
9. I took Casey the boy with the short hair to dinner last night.
10. Heather left Los Angeles on February 2 of that year

Language

Writing

Directions: Imagine you are touring the Grand Canyon on horseback. Use the flowchart to write some ideas for the beginning, middle, and end of a narrative. Use your imagination as well as any information you may already know about the Grand Canyon to help you.

Beginning

Middle

End

Directions: Imagine you are taking a tour of the Grand Canyon on horseback. Describe the experience, including details about how you feel and what the scenery looks like. Use your notes from page 26 to help you write your narrative paragraph.

Remember!

A strong narrative paragraph tells a story with a beginning, a middle, and an end.

Writing

Directions: Solve each problem.

1. Write the line length in centimeters.

____

2. Circle the best estimate for the weight of the object.

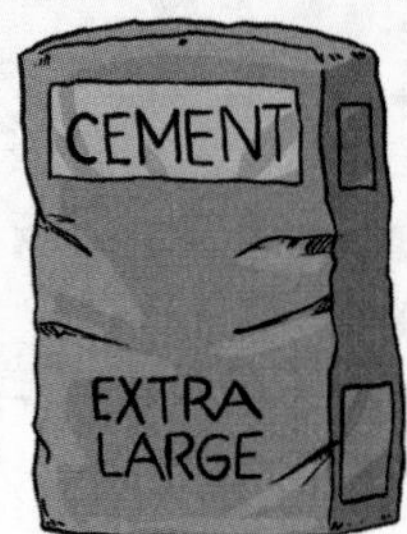

100 g

2 kg

5 kg

10 kg

3. How many millimeters are in 5 centimeters?

____

4. I put 700 mL of water in the jar. Then, I put a toy in the jar. How much water was displaced by the toy?

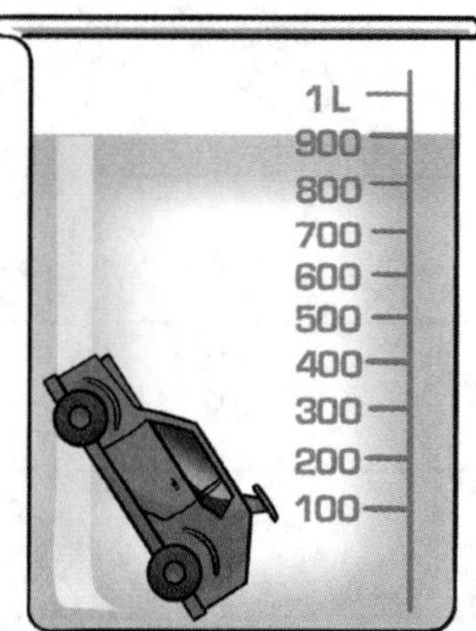

________ mL was displaced.

5. What unit of measure is used for volume?

____

6. Write the length in millimeters.

____

7. Dan's mass is double the mass of Tim, whose mass is 39 kg. What is Dan's mass?

____

8. How many full oil bottles can be poured into the bucket?

____

9. How many centimeters are in a meter?

____

Directions: Solve each problem.

1. Fill in the blanks for the time shown.

4:________

5. Fill in the blanks for the time shown.

7:________

2. Show 20 to 3 on both clocks.

6. Draw the time that is 10 minutes later.

3. Fill in the blanks for the time shown.

12:________

7. Draw the time that is 20 minutes later.

4. Draw the time that is 15 minutes later.

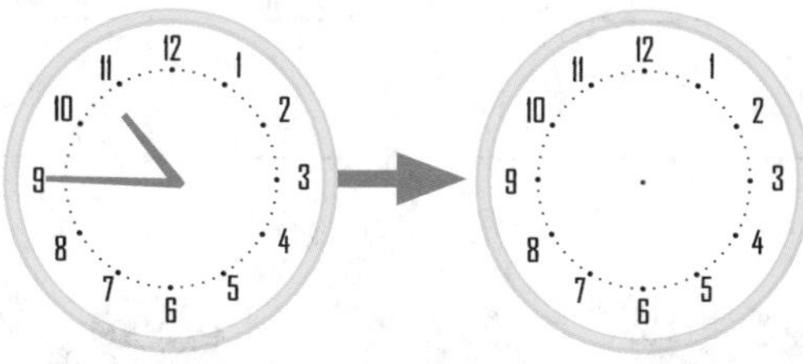

8. Draw the time that is 8 minutes later.

Mathematics

Problem Solving

Directions: Read the problem, and answer the questions.

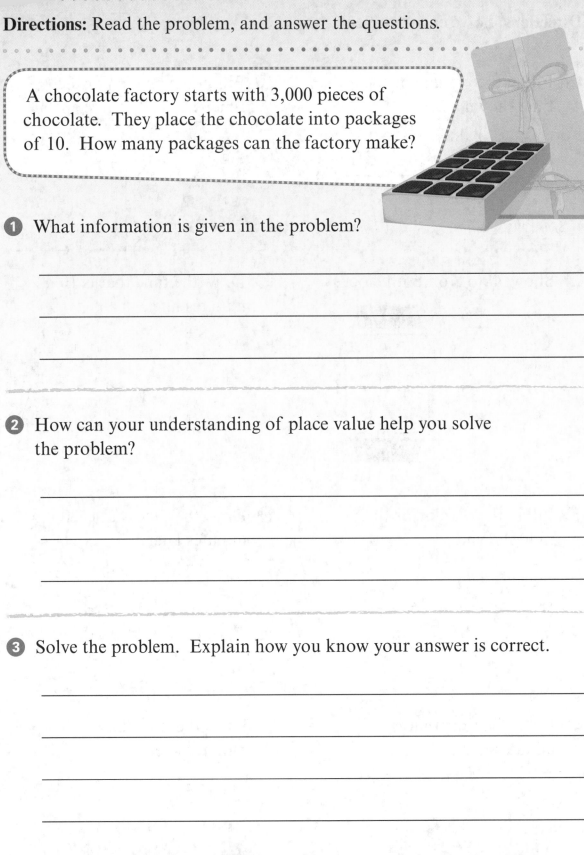

A chocolate factory starts with 3,000 pieces of chocolate. They place the chocolate into packages of 10. How many packages can the factory make?

1. What information is given in the problem?

2. How can your understanding of place value help you solve the problem?

3. Solve the problem. Explain how you know your answer is correct.

Directions: Read and solve each problem.

Problem 1

A toy factory starts with 4,000 toys. They place the toys into boxes of 100. How many boxes can the factory make?

List What You Know	Write Your Plan
Solve the Problem	**Look Back and Explain**

Problem 2

A bank stores $180,000 in stacks of $1,000 in a safe. How many stacks of $1,000 are in the safe?

List What You Know	Write Your Plan
Solve the Problem	**Look Back and Explain**

Social Studies

Directions: Read the definition of *authority*. Then, answer the questions.

> **authority:** the power or the right to make decisions or to control things

1. List five people who have some kind of authority.

___

___

___

2. Why do these people have authority?

___

___

3. Who might use their authority for good?

___

___

4. A bully has power, but no authority. If a bully were caught, he or she might be in trouble. How might a bully use power in a bad way?

___

___

___

5. Who has the authority to help change a bully's behavior?

___

___

Directions: Follow the steps in this experiment to discover how sound works.

What You Need

rubber bands

What to Do

1. What do you think sound is? How could you prove what you think?

____

____

2. Stretch a rubber band between your thumb and forefinger. Pluck it. Describe what happens.

____

____

3. Stretch the rubber band as tightly as you can. Pluck it. Describe the difference.

____

____

4. Repeat steps 2 and 3 with rubber bands of different sizes. What is the same? What is different?

____

____

____

____

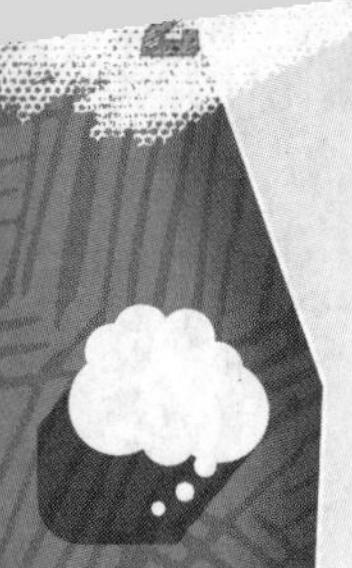

Critical Thinking

Directions: How many different words can you make using only the letters in the word *authority*? Write as many as you can on the lines. Then, write three sentences that use the words you created.

AUTHORITY

1.

2.

3.

Directions: Play with a partner. Use small objects to mark your spots on the game board. Take turns rolling a number cube. Move the number of spaces that you roll. If you land on a space with a type of person on it, explain how he or she has authority. The first person to reach the finish wins.

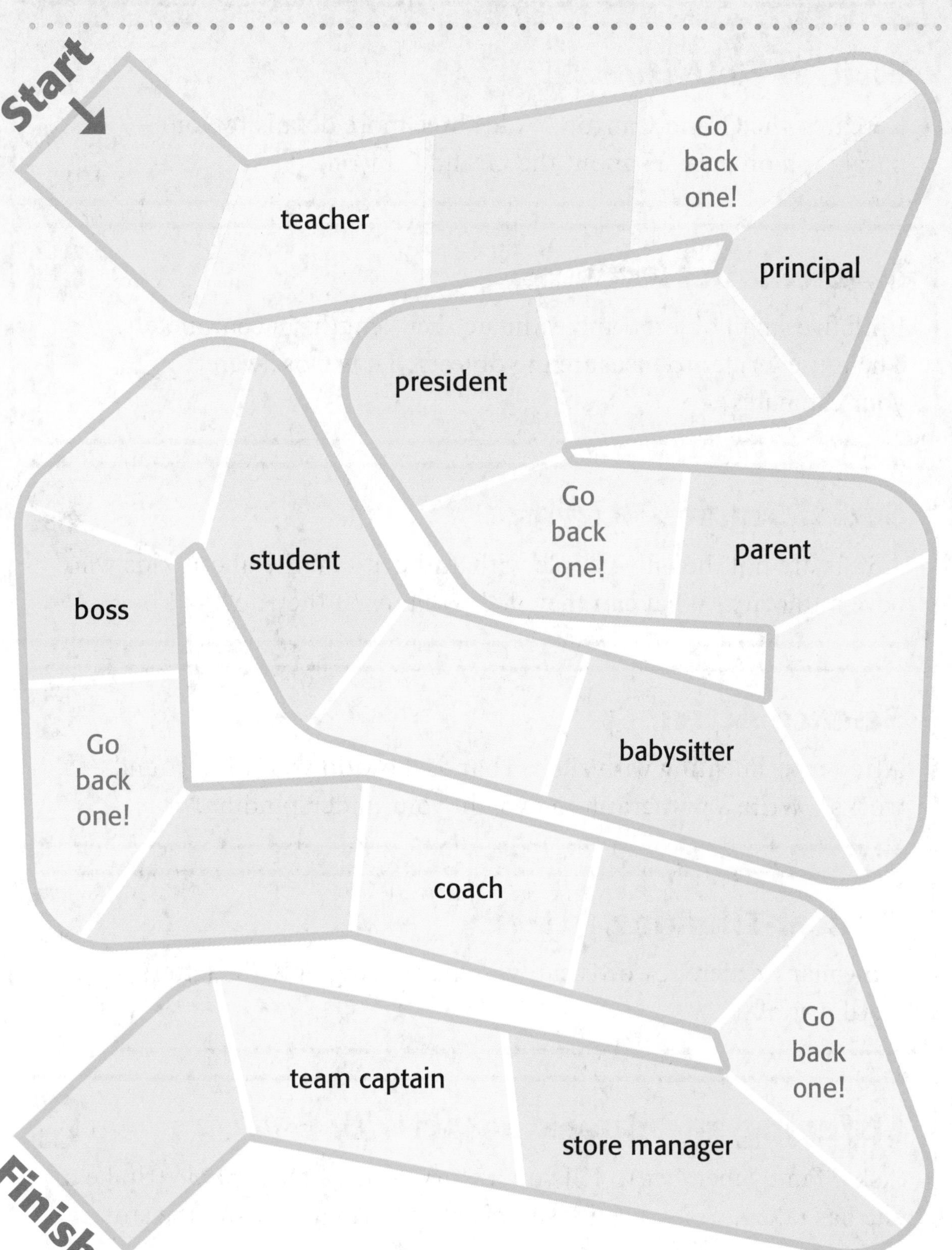

Game

Spelling Activity

Think of three more words that have *ou* in them. For each word, determine whether the letters make the /ow/ or /aw/ sound.

Writing Activity

Research the Grand Canyon. Add three more details to your paragraph on page 27 about the Grand Canyon.

Mathematics Activity

Find five small objects, and estimate their lengths in centimeters. Then, use a ruler to measure the objects. How close were your estimates?

Social Studies Activity

Adults are not the only people with authority. Write about kids who have authority. What can they do? What can't they do?

Science Activity

After experimenting with rubber bands, how do you think sound works? Write a paragraph to explain your understanding.

Critical-Thinking Activity

How many different words can you make using only the letters in the word *power*?

Listening-and-Speaking Activity

Ask a family member to tell you a story about a memorable trip he or she has taken. Ask questions to clarify information from the story.

Directions: Read the text, and answer the questions.

Reading

Let the Force Be with You

What happens if you hold a pencil in your hand and then let go of it? You probably don't need to try this experiment to know that the pencil will fall to the ground. This happens because gravity is at work. Gravity is a force that pulls objects towards one another. Everything has gravity. So why are things always drawn to the ground instead of to each other? Larger objects have more gravity than smaller objects do. So Earth's pull is stronger than any other object on Earth. The sun is much larger than Earth. That means the sun's gravity is much stronger. That's the reason Earth orbits the sun. The sun's gravity pulls Earth toward it.

1. Would reading the first sentence help the reader preview the text?
   - (A) Yes. It introduces the topic.
   - (B) Yes. It describes what will happen.
   - (C) Yes. It provides a good deal of information.
   - (D) No. The topic sentence comes later in the text.

2. Which index entry would help a reader find this information?
   - (A) experiments
   - (B) gravity
   - (C) sun, the
   - (D) Earth, the

3. Which syllable is stressed in the word *gravity*?
   - (A) the first syllable
   - (B) the second syllable
   - (C) the third syllable
   - (D) none of the above

4. A synonym for *experiment* is
   - (A) game.
   - (B) test.
   - (C) outfit.
   - (D) book.

5. What is the author's purpose?
   - (A) to persuade
   - (B) to entertain
   - (C) to confuse
   - (D) to inform

Reading

Directions: Read the text, and answer the questions.

The Choice

When school was over on Monday, Donna flew to the music room. She wanted to choose an instrument so she could play in the band. When she arrived, she said, "Hi, Mrs. Taylor. I'm here to choose an instrument."

"I'm so glad you're interested in the band, Donna," said Mrs. Taylor. "Is there any instrument that particularly interests you? The flute? The violin?"

"I heard that the clarinet is easy, and I like the way it sounds," Donna answered. "That's the instrument I'd like."

"Well, the clarinet isn't especially difficult, but it takes daily practice to learn it well," said Mrs. Taylor. "Our first band practice will be one week from today."

1. Which sentence gives the best preview of the text?
   - (A) the first sentence
   - (B) the second sentence
   - (C) the third sentence
   - (D) the fourth sentence

2. Which words share the same suffix?
   - (A) *interested* and *answered*
   - (B) *wanted* and *instrument*
   - (C) *answered* and *especially*
   - (D) *instrument* and *trumpet*

3. A synonym for *difficult* is
   - (A) easy.
   - (B) simple.
   - (C) uncomplicated.
   - (D) challenging.

4. *Donna flew to the music room* is an example of
   - (A) literal language.
   - (B) figurative language.
   - (C) formal language.
   - (D) misleading language.

Directions: Write your own definition of each word. Use a dictionary if you don't know its meaning. Then, cover the word, and write it in the box.

ABC Spelling

1. lotion
2. station
3. vacation
4. action
5. location
6. question
7. vision
8. decision

Directions: Write the correct word to complete each sentence.

1. The giant couldn't ______________________ down fast enough.
   (*clime, clim, climb*)

2. Tinker Bell was a ______________________.
   (*ferry, fairy, farely*)

3. Someday, he'd like to sail the seven ______________________.
   (*sees, sea, seas*)

4. You could ______________________ at the amazing views.
   (*stair, stare, start*)

5. You ______________________ not want to start a forest fire!
   (*would, wood*)

6. Kira and Lina like to shop the ______________________ in the city.
   (*sails, sales*)

7. Brody hurt his knee because he was running quickly

   and he ______________.
   (*fall, fell*)

Directions: Read the information about Beethoven. Then, complete the table.

Beethoven was a musician and composer who lived from 1770 to 1827. He composed nine symphonies and dozens of pieces of music for piano and string quartets. Beethoven was completely deaf when he composed his most important works. Students from elementary school to college study his music.

Should Beethoven's music be taught today? Write a few notes in each column about why someone would answer "yes" or "no."

Yes	No

Writing

Directions: Explain why you think Beethoven's music should or should not be taught today. Use your notes from page 41 to help you write your opinion paragraph.

Remember!

A strong opinion paragraph includes:

- an introductory sentence stating your opinion
- details that support your opinion
- a concluding sentence that restates your opinion

Directions: Solve each problem.

1. Calculate the perimeter of a square with 3 cm sides.

3 cm

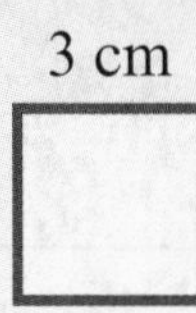

____

2. Calculate the perimeter of the rectangle.

3 cm

6 cm

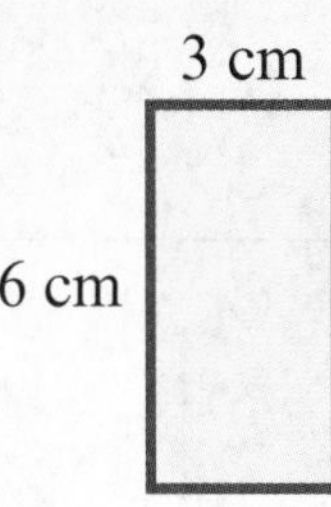

____

3. Calculate the perimeter of a square with 2 cm sides.

2 cm

____

4. Find the perimeter of a figure with these 4 sides: 3 cm, 5 cm, 7 cm, 4 cm.

____

5. Calculate the perimeter of a regular pentagon with 3 inch sides.

____

6. Calculate the perimeter of a square with 7 cm sides.

7 cm

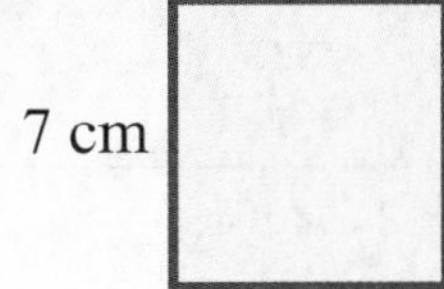

____

7. Calculate the perimeter of the object below.

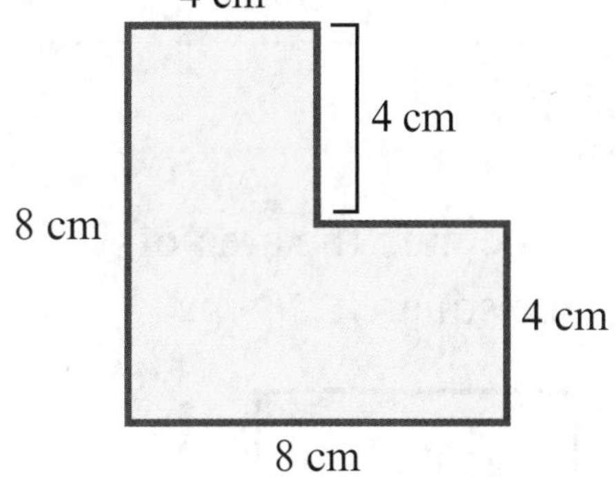

____

Mathematics

Directions: Solve each problem.

1. Calculate the area of the square.

4 cm

____

2. What is the area of a rectangle that measures 4 cm by 12 cm?

____

3. The area of a flower bed is 12 m^2 and the area of the grass is 24 m^2. What is their combined area?

____

4. Calculate the area of the square.

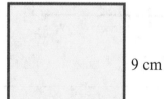

9 cm

____

5. Would you use square inches or square feet to measure the area of a bedroom?

____

6. My garden bed has an area of 18 m^2. I planted 10 m^2 with peas. What area is left?

____

7. Calculate the area of the square.

5 cm

____

8. What is the area of a rectangle that measures 3 cm by 9 cm?

____

9. One side of a square is 10 cm. What is the area?

____

Directions: Look at the example. Then, solve the problem.

Example: Kato wants to climb a mountain that is 15,000 feet above sea level. At the first stop, he climbs to 3,898 feet. At the second stop, Kato is 8,945 feet above sea level. How much farther must he climb to reach the top of the mountain?

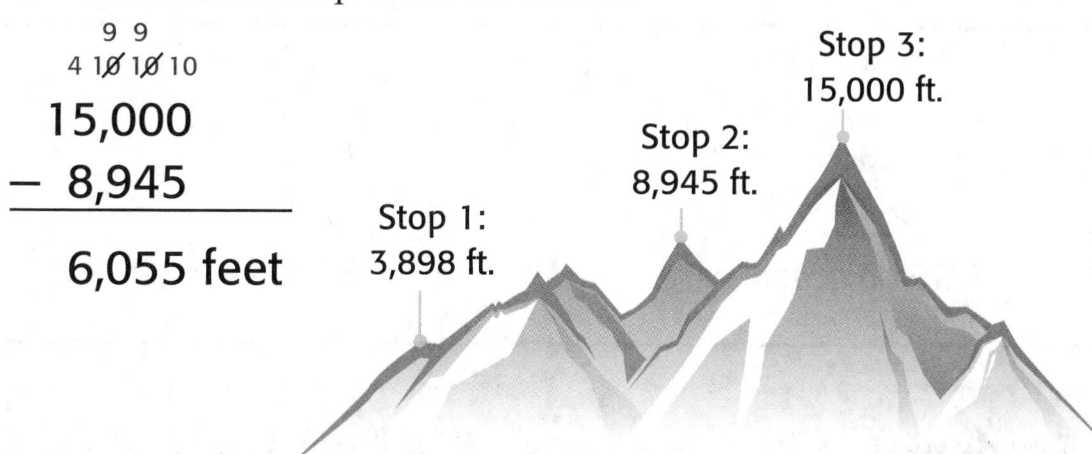

A family takes a road trip and drives a total of 2,500 kilometers. The family leaves home and drives 746 kilometers the first week. By the end of the second week, the family has driven a total of 1,894 kilometers. How many kilometers does the family drive during the third week?

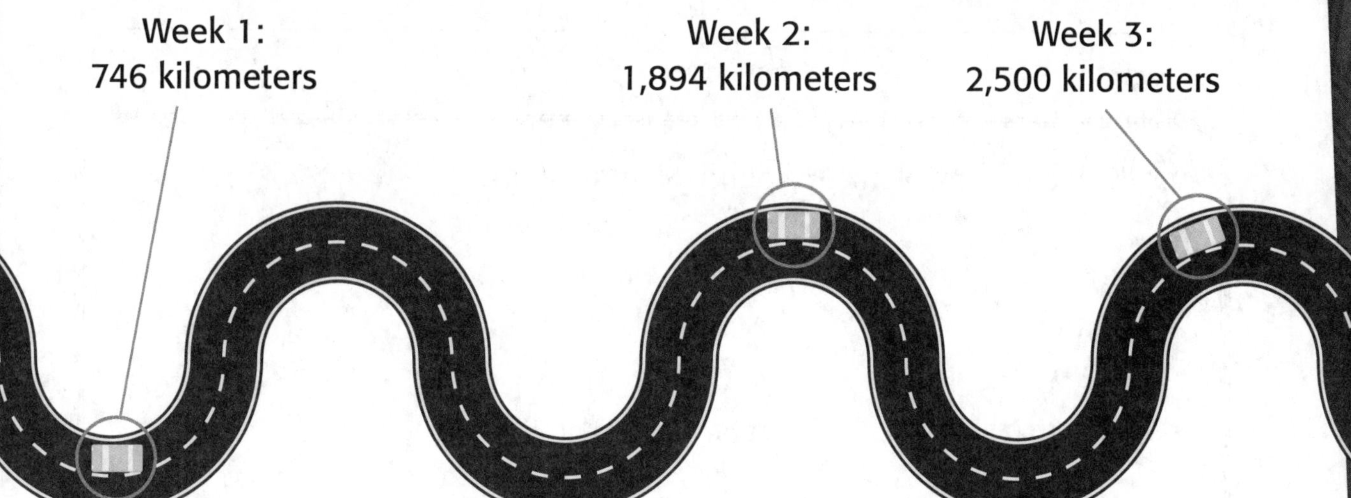

Problem Solving

Directions: Two students solved a problem two different ways. Explain what error each student made.

1. A juicing company purchases 3,849 oranges from a local farmer. The farmer began the day with 8,186 oranges. How many oranges does the farmer have left?

Student 1	Student 2
$\begin{array}{r} 8{,}186 \\ -\ 3{,}849 \\ \hline 12{,}035 \end{array}$ oranges	$\begin{array}{r} 8{,}186 \\ -\ 3{,}849 \\ \hline 5{,}743 \end{array}$ oranges

Student 1

____

____

____

____

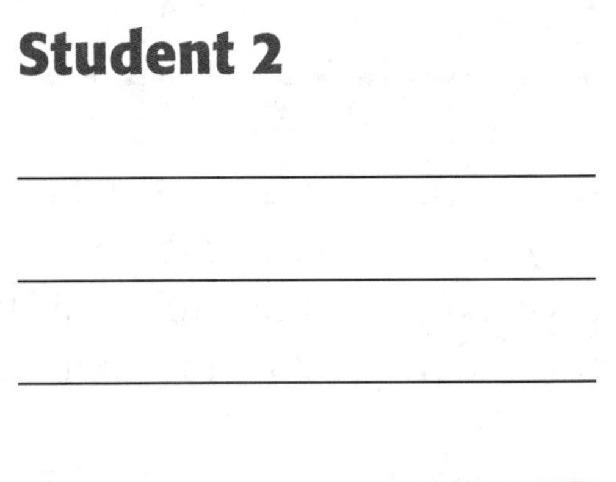

2. Solve the problem. Explain your strategy.

Directions: Rules and laws exist to help people to live together peacefully. Make a list of the laws from your community.

1.

• ______	• ______
• ______	• ______
• ______	• ______

2. How do these laws help people?

______

______

______

______

Social Studies

Science

Directions: Follow the steps in this experiment to discover how erosion works.

What You Need

- newspaper
- two trays
- jug with spout
- water
- block
- soil

What to Do

1. Cover your table with newspaper. Put soil 4 cm (1.5 in.) deep in one tray. Pat the soil down firmly so that it is level.

2. Put one side of the soil tray on a block so that it is on a slope. Put the empty tray under the end of the soil tray. This tray will catch the water.

3. Carefully pour a small stream of water into the top of the soil tray. Stop pouring when water reaches the bottom of the tray. Draw and label a diagram.

4. Pour more water into the tray until you notice another change. Then, draw and label a diagram.

Directions: How much can you recall from the text on page 41? Complete the web to show what you remember. Then, reread the text, and add details to your web in a different color.

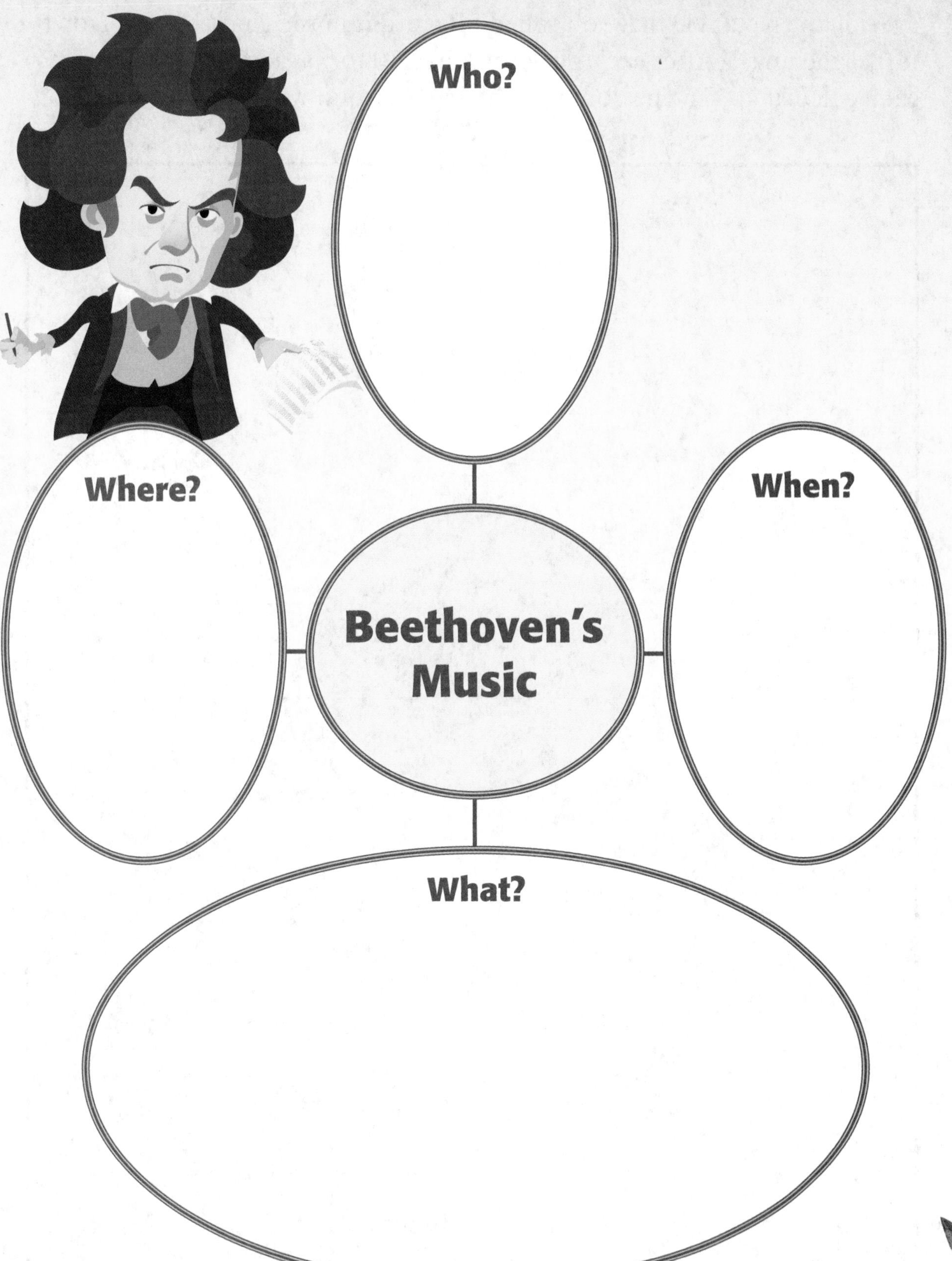

Critical Thinking

Game

Directions: Play with a partner. Take turns rolling two number cubes. One number cube represents the length of a rectangle. The other represents its width. For example, if you roll a 3 and a 4, you have a rectangle with a length of 3 units and a width of 4 units. Calculate the area of the rectangle that you rolled. Record it in the chart below. Don't forget the units! After each player has had 10 turns, add the areas you each calculated. The person with the highest total wins.

Player 1	Player 2
Total:	**Total:**

Writing Activity

Review your writing on page 42. Consider what people who disagree with your opinion might say. Add points to address their arguments.

Mathematics Activity

Estimate the area of your living room. Then, use the tape measure to measure it. Calculate the actual area. How close was your estimate?

Problem-Solving Activity

Imagine a family trip to a place of interest. Create a word problem related to the problem on page 45. How is your word problem similar to and different from the problem on that page?

Social Studies Activity

Choose a law from page 47. Draw a picture to show the law at work. Write a caption to explain how this law helps people live peacefully together.

Science Activity

Review the experiment from page 48. What might happen if you changed the amount of soil, the angle of the slope, the amount of water, or another variable? Repeat the experiment, changing only one variable, and record the results.

Listening-and-Speaking Activity

Tell a family member what you observed in the science experiment.

Directions: Read the text, and answer the questions.

Reading

Tasty Breads

There are many different kinds of sandwiches, and there are also many different kinds of bread. One delicious kind of bread is pita (PEE-tuh). Pita is a round, flat bread. It is from the Middle East, but it is very popular all over the world. Pita has a hollow center. When you cut a pita in half, you can fill it. That is why pita is sometimes called pocket bread. Another type of bread, called the baguette, comes from France. Baguettes are long, thin loaves of bread. They are crusty on the outside and soft on the inside. Baguettes are great for subs and other long sandwiches. There are many other varieties of bread, too. Which do you like best?

1. Why is pita sometimes called *pocket bread*?
   - (A) It is from the Middle East.
   - (B) It is crusty on the outside.
   - (C) It has a hollow center.
   - (D) It is flat.

2. Which sentence is NOT true?
   - (A) Baguettes are good bread for subs.
   - (B) Pita comes from France.
   - (C) Baguettes are long and thin.
   - (D) A pita is round.

3. Which is NOT a compound word?
   - (A) outside
   - (B) inside
   - (C) sometimes
   - (D) sandwich

4. Which words are synonyms?
   - (A) *tasty* and *delicious*
   - (B) *hollow* and *crusty*
   - (C) *popular* and *thin*
   - (D) *pocket* and *center*

5. What is the tone of the text?
   - (A) informative
   - (B) comical
   - (C) opinionated
   - (D) uncertain

Directions: Read the text, and answer the questions.

Reading

Keeping Score

It was the day before Carrie's birthday. Her parents had purchased tickets to a baseball game, and Carrie couldn't wait. Baseball was her favorite sport. She was even on her school's softball team. At practice, she told her coach how excited she was to go to an actual major-league game.

"Bring a score card so you can remember everything," the coach said.

"But I've never used a score card," Carrie said. "I don't know how."

"It's not difficult," the coach said. "I can teach you if you're interested."

"Thanks!" Carrie said. "I'd really like to learn."

The coach showed Carrie how to record statistics on a score card. Soon, she understood. She was ready for the game.

1. What does Carrie learn to do?
   - Ⓐ throw a baseball
   - Ⓑ use a score card
   - Ⓒ catch a baseball
   - Ⓓ buy tickets to a game

2. What is the setting?
   - Ⓐ the bus
   - Ⓑ softball practice
   - Ⓒ Carrie's house
   - Ⓓ choir rehearsal

3. Which word makes a new word by adding the prefix *un*–?
   - Ⓐ sure
   - Ⓑ had
   - Ⓒ wait
   - Ⓓ not

4. Which is a synonym for *actual*?
   - Ⓐ sharp
   - Ⓑ fun
   - Ⓒ big
   - Ⓓ real

5. *Carrie couldn't wait* is
   - Ⓐ onomatopoeia.
   - Ⓑ a simile.
   - Ⓒ a hyperbole.
   - Ⓓ a metaphor.

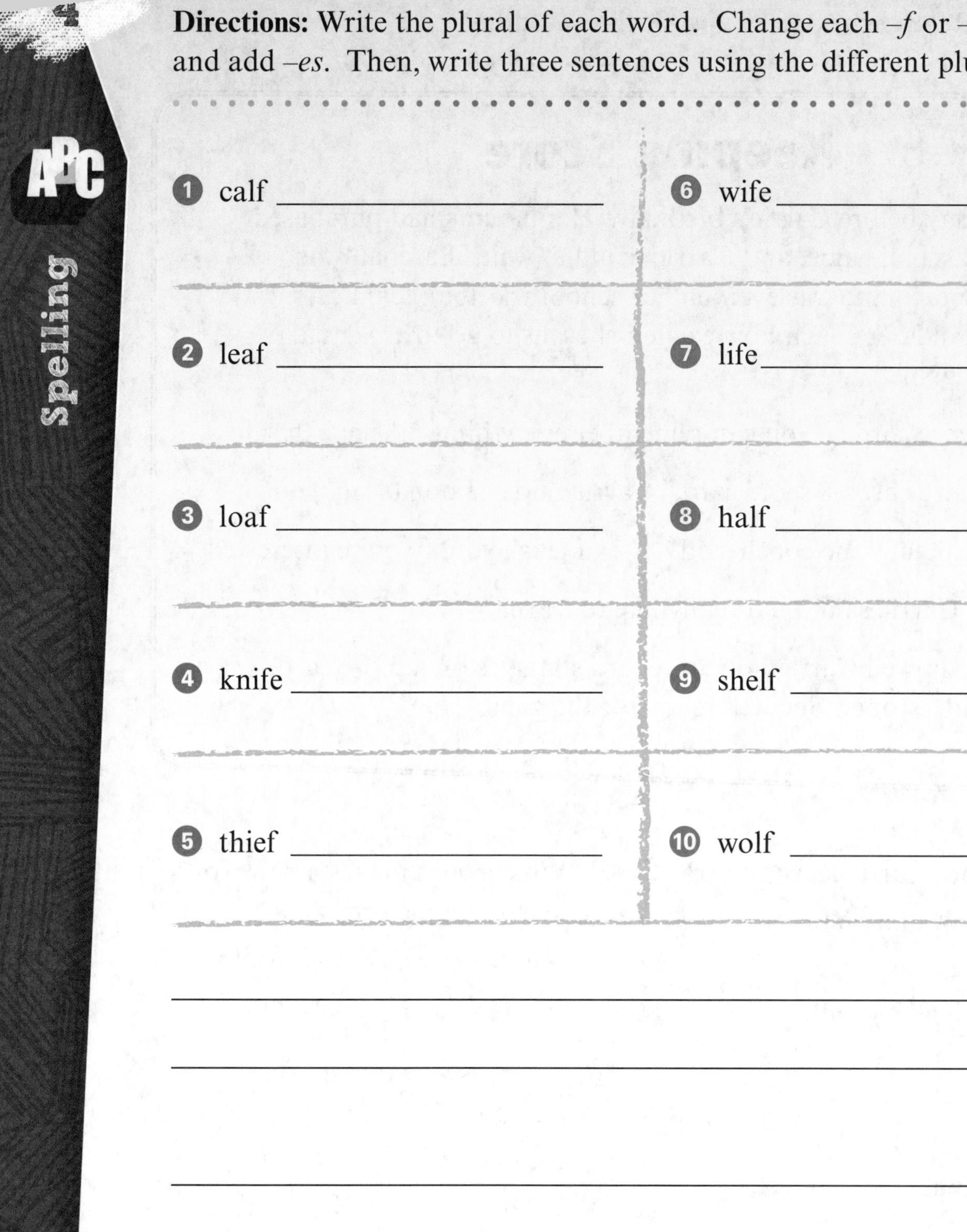

Directions: Write the plural of each word. Change each *–f* or *–fe* to a *–v* and add *–es*. Then, write three sentences using the different plural words.

1. calf ____________________
2. leaf ____________________
3. loaf ____________________
4. knife ____________________
5. thief ____________________
6. wife ____________________
7. life ____________________
8. half ____________________
9. shelf ____________________
10. wolf ____________________

Spelling

Directions: Answer each question.

1. Circle the proper nouns in the sentence below.

   Matteo and Jesse like to take the train to the city.

2. Circle the common noun in the sentence below.

   Ford produced affordable cars.

3. Circle the proper nouns in the sentence below.

   Springfield is smaller than Chicago.

4. Circle the proper nouns in the sentence below.

   Judy Garland sang a song in a movie called "Meet Me in St. Louis."

5. Circle the common nouns in the sentence below.

   Neo and Ellie tied ribbons on their bikes.

6. Circle the common noun in the sentence below.

   Colton likes kicking the football.

7. Circle the proper nouns in the sentence below.

   Many CBS television shows take place in Los Angeles.

Writing

Directions: Think of a time you played kickball. Write your thoughts about that game in the right column. If you have not played kickball, use your imagination to write your notes. Then, put stars by four to six ideas you would like to include in a personal narrative about playing kickball.

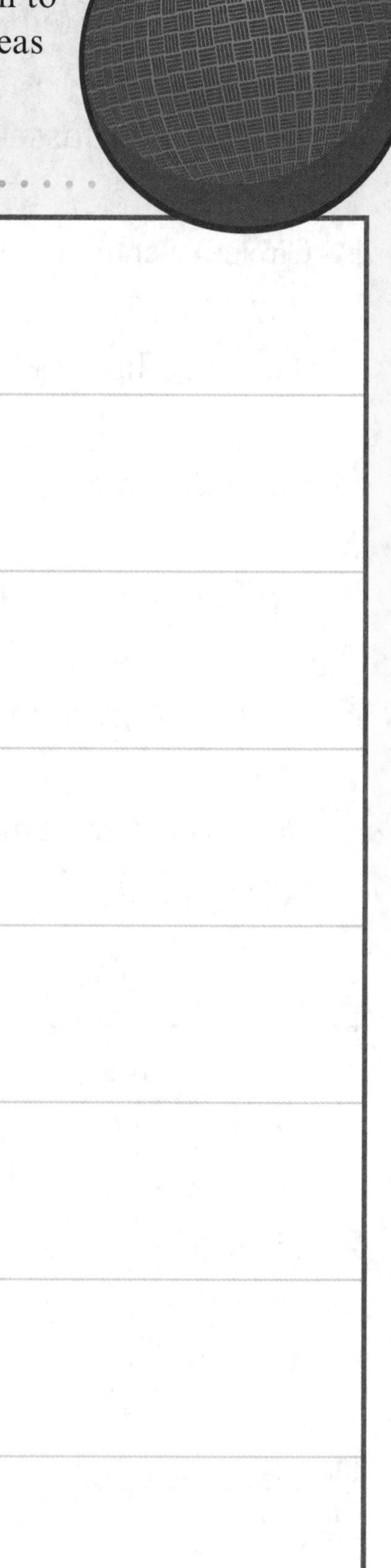

Directions: Write a narrative about a time you played kickball. Describe the experience, including details about whom you played with and how the game went. Use the notes from page 56 to help you.

Remember!

A strong personal narrative:

- is about you
- has a beginning, a middle, and an end
- sounds like a story

Directions: Solve each problem.

1. Which shape shows the same fraction as the example?

Example: 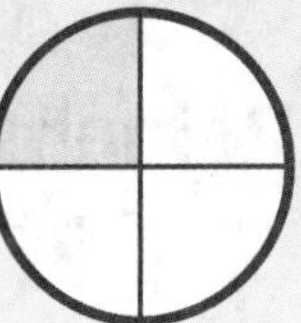

(A) 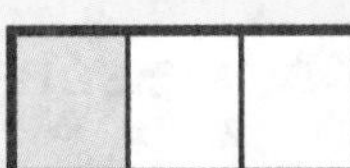

(B) 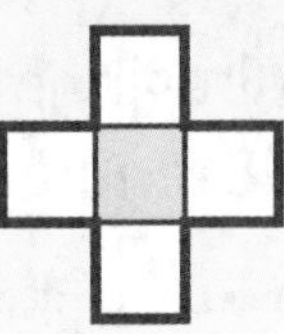

(C) 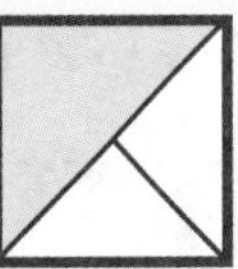

(D) 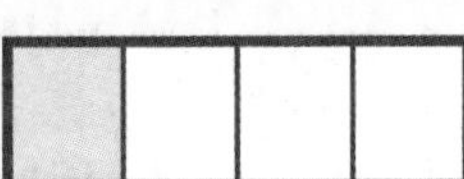

2. Show the amount shaded as a fraction and a decimal.

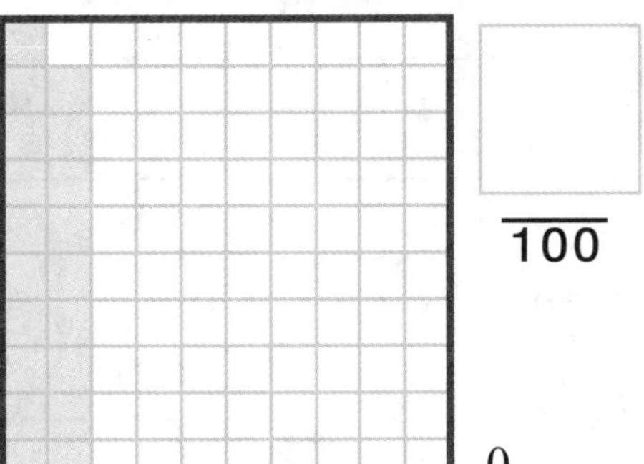

3. What fraction must be added to $\frac{3}{4}$ of a pizza to make 1 whole pizza?

____

4. Write 0.3 as a fraction.

____

5. What is $\frac{1}{6}$ of 36?

____

6. Write 0.62 as a fraction.

____

7. Circle the shape that shows the same fraction as the example.

Example: 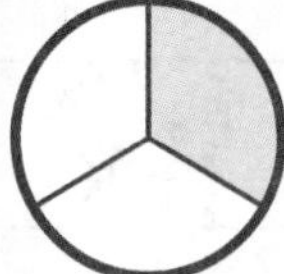

(A) 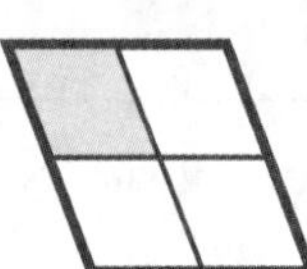

(B) 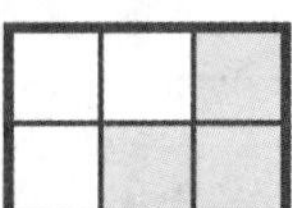

(C) 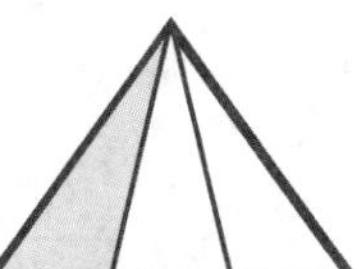

(D) 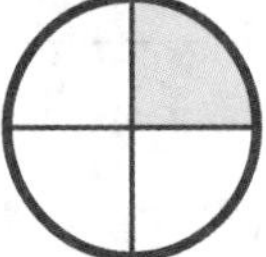

Directions: Solve each problem.

1. Write 0.25 as a fraction.

____

2. What fraction is shaded?

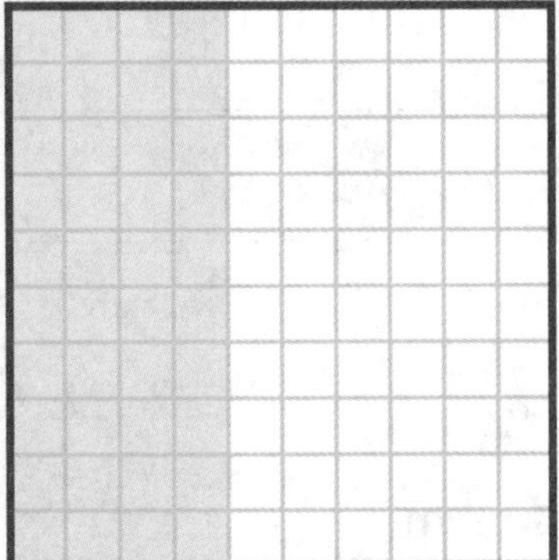

____

3. Fill in the missing fraction.

$\frac{1}{8}$, $\frac{2}{8}$, $\frac{3}{8}$, __________, $\frac{5}{8}$

4. Fill in the missing fraction.

$\frac{6}{10}$, $\frac{7}{10}$, __________, $\frac{9}{10}$

5. Write 0.81 as a fraction.

____

6. Write 0.7 as a fraction.

____

7. There are 8 circles. Two of them are blue. Four of them are red. The rest are orange. What fraction of the circles are orange?

____

8. Write 0.47 as a fraction.

____

9. Write 0.33 as a fraction.

____

Mathematics

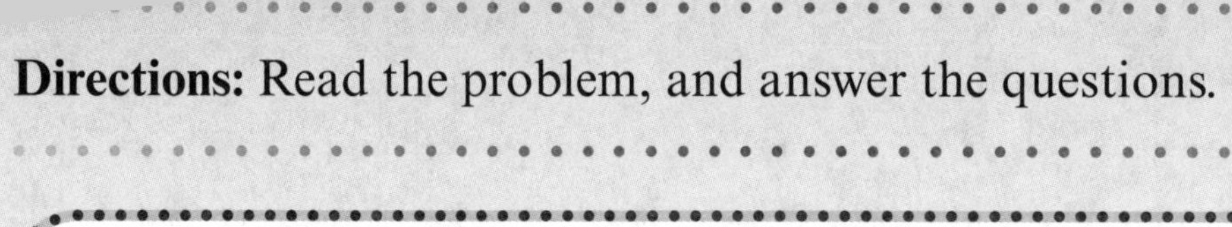

Directions: Read the problem, and answer the questions.

A cafeteria manager has 20 celery sticks to put into snack bags. Each snack bag must hold the same number of celery sticks. Find all the possible ways to prepare the snack bags. Identify the number of snack bags and the number of celery sticks in each bag.

Problem Solving

1. What do you need to find?

2. How can listing factors help you solve the problem?

3. Solve the problem. Explain your reasoning.

Directions: Read and solve the problem.

Problem: A cafeteria manager has 50 carrots to put into snack bags. Each snack bag must hold the same number of carrots. Find all the possible ways to prepare the snack bags. Identify the number of snack bags and the number of carrots in each bag.

List What You Know	Write Your Plan
Solve the Problem	**Look Back and Explain**

Social Studies

Directions: Read the passage from the Declaration of Independence. Look up any words you don't know. Then, rewrite it in your own words. Be sure to keep the meaning the same. Then, answer the questions.

> We hold these truths to be self-evident, that all men are created equal, that they are endowed by their Creator with certain unalienable Rights, that among these are Life, Liberty and the pursuit of Happiness.

____

____

____

____

1. Why might some words be capitalized?

____

____

2. Why do you think Thomas Jefferson included this sentence in the Declaration of Independence?

____

____

3. Why do people still think this passage is important?

____

____

____

Directions: Follow the steps in this experiment to discover how you can measure the wind.

What You Need

- ruler
- cardstock
- tape
- scissors
- half a ping-pong ball
- 30 cm of string

What to Do

1. Cut a semi-circle out of cardstock.
2. Use a small piece of tape to stick the end of the string to the inside of the ping pong ball.
3. Tape the other end of the string to the center of the semi-circle. Attach the semi-circle along the end of a ruler.
4. Take your wind gauge outside. Hold the ruler, pointing the semi-circle into the wind. Keep it level, still, and away from your body.
5. See how far the ping pong ball moves. Work out a way to record these results in the space below.

Science

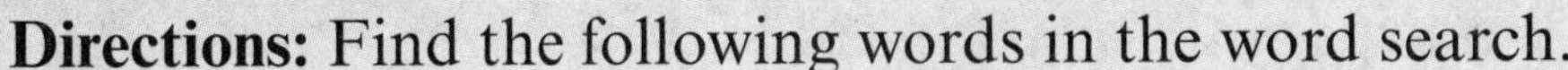

Directions: Find the following words in the word search.

- FREEDOM
- DEMOCRACY
- LIBERTY
- CONSTITUTION
- VALUES
- INDEPENDENCE

A	D	E	M	O	C	R	A	C	Y	G	C
D	V	E	P	C	L	A	Q	E	Z	R	O
F	A	C	C	M	I	T	C	B	U	D	N
N	L	H	S	L	I	B	E	R	T	Y	S
V	U	K	V	Y	F	E	J	G	W	H	T
Y	E	W	J	K	R	D	S	V	L	M	I
S	S	X	T	O	E	F	A	U	E	T	T
R	M	C	L	P	E	Q	R	T	S	K	U
C	O	N	T	S	D	T	U	T	I	O	T
U	H	N	D	E	O	Y	F	P	U	O	I
B	N	X	W	X	M	G	M	O	Y	I	O
O	D	Z	A	G	N	P	E	R	I	A	N
I	N	D	E	P	E	N	D	E	N	C	E

Critical Thinking

Directions: Work with a partner. Take turns rolling a number cube, two times per roll. The first roll tells you which column to look at. The second roll tells you which row to look at. Write your initials on the word you rolled, and read it aloud. For example, if you roll a 3 and then a 5, you would read *shelf*. The first person to match three words with its singular or plural form wins.

	1	2	3	4	5	6
1	calves	thief	mice	wolf	halves	life
2	tooth	knife	leaves	feet	wives	geese
3	shelves	selves	goose	teeth	woman	knives
4	children	loaves	people	thieves	foot	self
5	lives	half	shelf	child	calf	loaf
6	mouse	wife	women	wolves	person	leaf

Game

Spelling Activity

Find three other nouns where the singular form ends in *–f* and the plural form ends in *–ves*. Write a sentence using each one in your best cursive handwriting.

Writing Activity

Read your writing on page 57 aloud. Pay attention to any grammatical errors or parts of the writing that do not flow smoothly. Make revisions as needed.

Mathematics Activity

Choose two of the fractions from pages 58 and 59. Write them in different forms, draw pictures, and use objects to show the fractions in as many ways as you can.

Social Studies Activity

Research the Declaration of Independence. Why was it written? When was it written and to whom? What effect did the document have on the United States? Write a paragraph to answer these questions.

Science Activity

Take your wind gauge to different locations on different days. Record your results. Where do you observe the biggest differences?

Listening-and-Speaking Activity

Ask your family what the Declaration of Independence means to them. Discuss why it is important and how it affects people today.

Directions: Read the text, and answer the questions.

The Wonderful Web

The Internet is a very important part of our lives. Today's Internet lets people do things they could never do before. You can find recipes and advice. You can watch movies and TV shows. You can keep in touch with friends and family. The Internet is also a very good place to find information. Do you want to learn to speak a new language? There are websites that help you learn. There are websites that help you make sure your guitar is tuned correctly. Maybe you want to visit a museum. Many museums have websites that let you take virtual tours. The Internet has made it easy to find almost anything you want.

1. In which chapter would this text be located?
   - (A) Chapter 2: Learning Spanish
   - (B) Chapter 9: Popular TV Shows
   - (C) Chapter 5: Insects
   - (D) Chapter 7: The Internet

2. Which vowel sound is not in the word *museum*?
   - (A) short e
   - (B) long e
   - (C) short u
   - (D) long u

3. What is the tone of the text?
   - (A) humorous
   - (B) informative
   - (C) fearful
   - (D) negative

4. Based on the text, the phrase *keep in touch* means
   - (A) to touch and then keep items
   - (B) to keep items within reach
   - (C) to be able to touch an object
   - (D) to regularly communicate with others

Reading

Reading

Directions: Read the text, and answer the questions.

A Fun New Game

Alex walked to school every morning. He passed several stores on his way to school, but one of the more interesting shops was a video game store called GameBegin. Alex loved video games, so he sometimes stopped at the store. One day, he noticed a new game called *Time Travel*. Alex was excited—the game looked like so much fun! He decided he wanted the game. But it was expensive, and Alex knew his parents would not buy such an expensive game for him. He would have to save his money. It would take time to save up the money, and Alex was afraid the store would not have the game once he was ready to buy it. Then, Alex had an idea. "My birthday's coming up next month," he thought. "I'll ask for the game as a birthday present, and then Mom and Dad will get it for me."

1. Which game does Alex want to buy?
   - (A) GameBegin
   - (B) Expensive Game
   - (C) Time Travel
   - (D) all of the above

2. The dialogue in the text shows that Alex is
   - (A) careful.
   - (B) hopeful.
   - (C) cunning.
   - (D) sophisticated.

3. *Several* means
   - (A) a few.
   - (B) one.
   - (C) many.
   - (D) more than a few.

4. In this text, *coming up* means
   - (A) far away.
   - (B) visiting.
   - (C) rising.
   - (D) about to happen.

Directions: A superlative is the most extreme. For example, that mouse might be *small*, but this one is the *smallest*. *Smallest* is a superlative. Write each word as a superlative. Then, write two sentences using at least one of these superlatives in each.

1. wider ______________________
2. hotter ______________________
3. crazy ______________________
4. pretty ______________________
5. funnier ______________________
6. tiny ______________________
7. larger ______________________
8. nicer ______________________
9. calm ______________________
10. happier ______________________

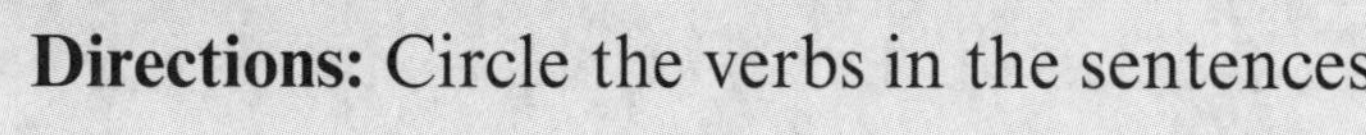

Directions: Circle the verbs in the sentences.

1. Many Beijing visitors tour the nearby Great Wall.
2. Eliana competed in and won Mr. Petersen's spelling contest.
3. Some people celebrate with gifts.
4. Chi misses his friends and relatives in Vietnam.
5. People named the delicious idea after him, the Earl of Sandwich.
6. You can ride the roller coaster for a nickel!
7. There are thousands of tales about different "Cinderellas" who marry princes.
8. The elephant lived in a zoo in England.
9. Sasha swam five laps in the pool and walked around the track.
10. Every morning, Maya eats a healthy breakfast.

Directions: Study the idea web. The notes are for an informative/explanatory paragraph about what comets look like. Place check marks in the circles with information that supports the main topic.

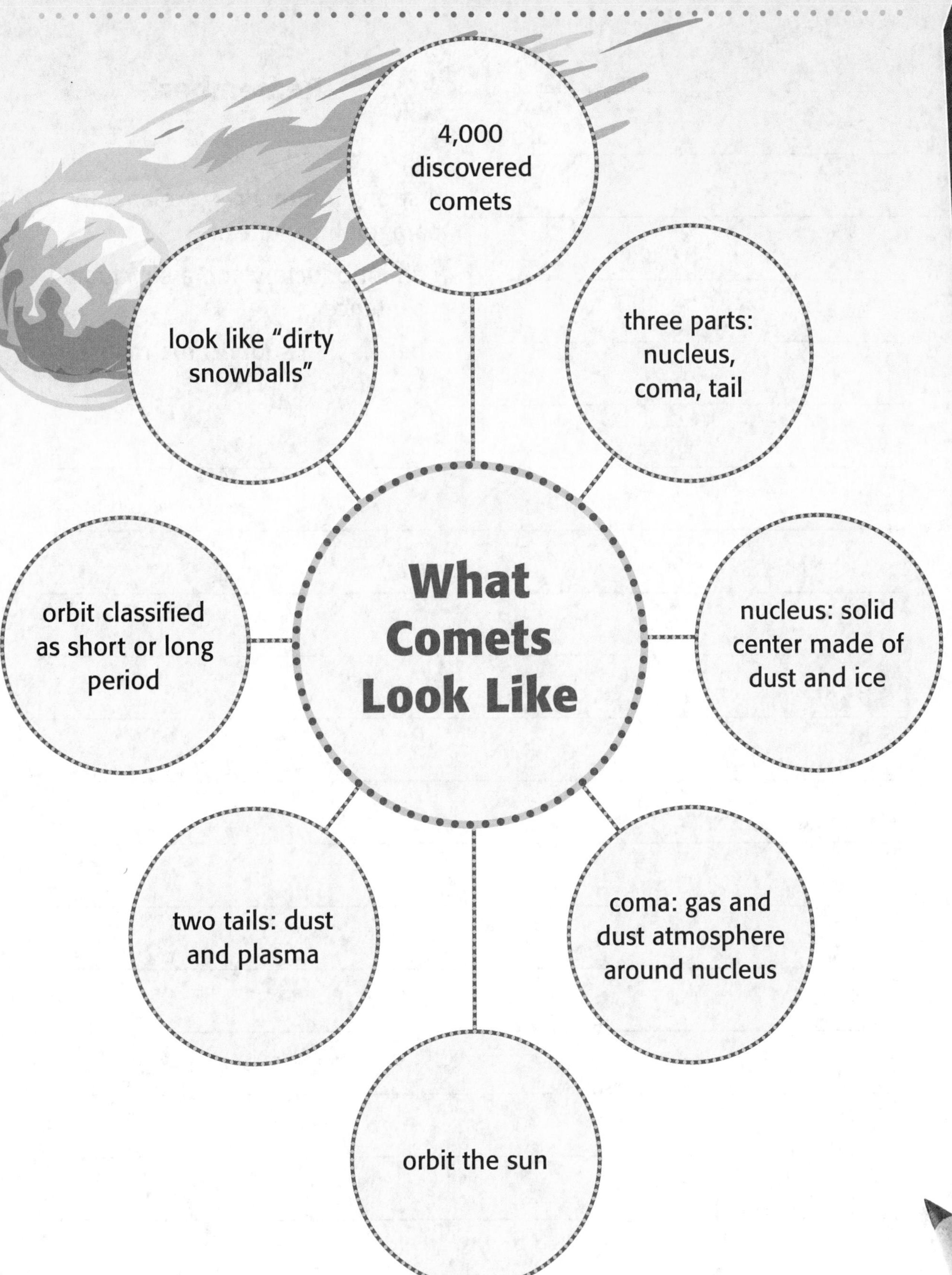

Directions: Write an informative/explanatory paragraph describing what a comet looks like. Include facts that tell about the parts of a comet. Use the web from page 71 to help you.

Remember!

A strong informative/explanatory paragraph includes:

- an introductory and a concluding sentence
- details that support the main idea

Directions: Solve each problem.

1. Round 423 to the nearest ten and hundred.

ten	
hundred	

2. Round 872 to the nearest ten and hundred.

ten	
hundred	

3. Round 132 to the nearest ten.

____

4. Round 1,874 to the nearest hundred.

____

5. Round 457 to the nearest hundred.

____

6. Round 789 to the nearest ten.

____

7. Round 372 to the nearest hundred.

____

8. Round 4,832 to the nearest ten, hundred, and thousand.

ten	
hundred	
thousand	

9. Round 156 to the nearest hundred.

____

10. Round 1,275 to the nearest hundred.

____

Mathematics

Directions: Solve each problem.

1. Patrick has swimming lessons 3 times a week. Each practice is half an hour long. How much time does he spend in 4 weeks at swimming lessons?

____

2. If you multiply me by 8, the product is 96. What number am I?

____

3. Kelly's mom pays her $4.00 an hour to babysit her little sister. How much money will she make in 4 weeks if she watches her sister 3 hours every week?

____

4. Sheila bought 3 dozen eggs. How many eggs did she buy?

____

5. $\frac{1}{5}$ of 35 = 7, so $\frac{3}{5}$ of 35 = ☐

6. Draw 9 triangles. Color $\frac{2}{3}$ of them yellow. Color the rest blue. How many are blue?

____

7. Follow the pattern in the first circle to complete the second circle.

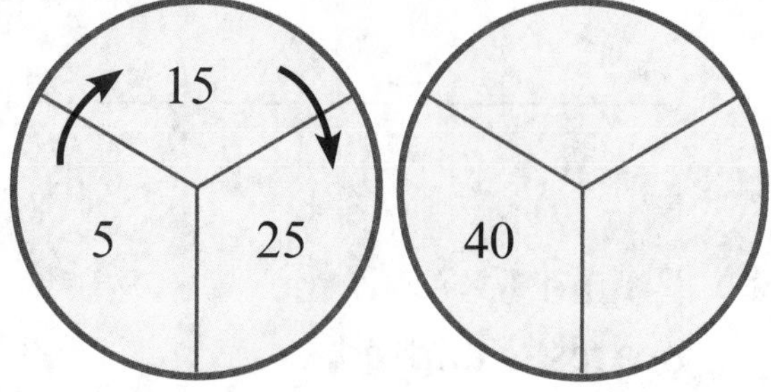

8. Yi Min's school is six miles from her home. Yi Min traveled back and forth to school on the bus all five days last week. How many total miles did Yi Min ride on the school bus during the week?

____

Directions: Look at the example. Then, solve the problem using the graph.

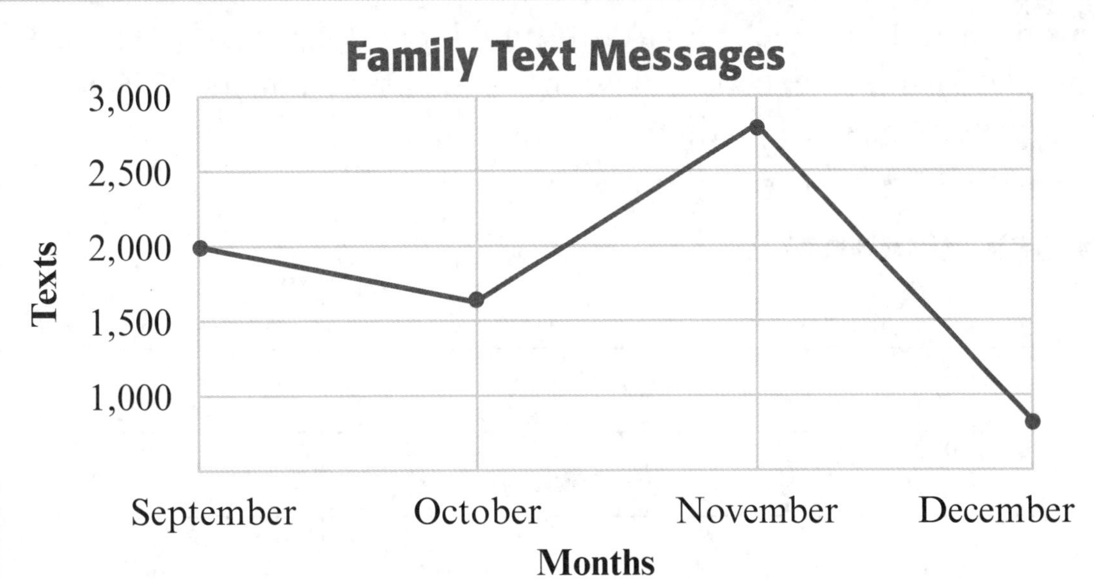

Example: Members of a family of four each send about the same number of text messages per month. Use the information in the line graph to estimate the number of texts each family member sent during the months of September and October.

Month	Expression Using Estimates	Estimated Texts Per Person
September	2,000 ÷ 4	500
October	1,600 ÷ 4	400

Use the information in the line graph to estimate the number of texts each family member sent during the months of November and December.

Month	Expression Using Estimates	Estimated Texts Per Person
November		
December		

Problem Solving

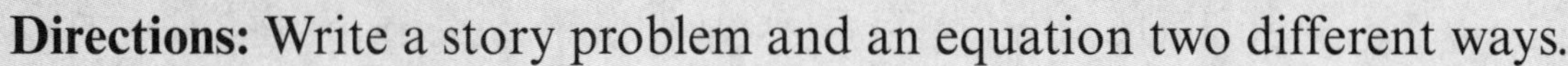

Directions: Write a story problem and an equation two different ways.

Problem Solving

1. Use the numbers 50, 70, and 3,500 to write a multiplication story problem and a division story problem. Represent each of your story problems with an equation. Use the same three numbers for each story problem and equation.

Story Problem 1

____

____

____

____

Story Problem 2

____

____

____

____

2. How did you determine which number to use for the product and which numbers to use for the factors? Where are the product and factors in the division problem?

____

____

____

Directions: Study the map below. Then, answer the questions.

VENEZUELA
GUYANA
SURINAME
French Guiana (FRANCE)
COLOMBIA
Galapagos Islands (ECUADOR)
ECUADOR
BRAZIL
PERU
BOLIVIA
PARAGUAY
CHILE
URUGUAY
ARGENTINA
N
W
E
S
0
500 Mi

Social Studies

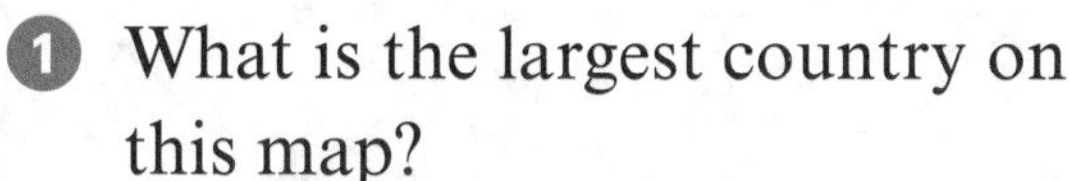

1. What is the largest country on this map?

   ____

3. What country lies west of Venezuela?

   ____

2. If you travel south from Paraguay, what country will you be in next?

   ____

4. Which is the best estimate for the length of South America, north to south?

   (A) 500 miles
   (B) 1,000 miles
   (C) 5,000 miles

Directions: Follow the steps in this experiment to discover how you can grow your own lunch.

Science

What You Need

- seeds (alfalfa or cress)
- paper plate
- cotton
- water

What to Do

1. Line the bottom of the plate with damp cotton. Sprinkle the seeds over the cotton. Cover any exposed seeds with more damp cotton.
2. Leave the plate in a light, warm, and airy place. Keep the cotton damp (but not wet). Watch the seeds grow for three weeks.
3. Draw what you see each week:

Week 1
Week 2
Week 3

Directions: Every mini-grid must have one each of the numbers 1–6. Every column must have one each of the numbers 1–6. Every row must have one each of the numbers 1–6.

3					
6					2
	1		5		
		3	2		6
1		4	6		
					4

Critical Thinking

Game

Directions: Play with a partner. Take turns rolling three number cubes. Use the values on each cube to create a three-digit number. Write it in your chart. Then, round that number to the nearest ten and the nearest hundred. After each player has had 5 turns, add up your tens and hundreds columns. The person with the highest score wins.

Player 1: ______________________________

Number	Ten	Hundred
	Total:	Total:

Player 2: ______________________________

Number	Ten	Hundred
	Total:	Total:

Spelling Activity

Write a series of sentences using superlatives. Example: *This puppy is small. This puppy is smaller. That puppy is the smallest.*

Writing Activity

Research more about comets. Add three more details to your paragraph on page 72.

Mathematics Activity

Look for sets of objects in your home or in stores. Determine how many ways each set can be broken into different fractions.

Problem-Solving Activity

Ask each family member to tell you the number of text messages they sent in one day. Estimate how many they each send over the course of a week. Add all of these together to determine the family's total. Use this to estimate the number of messages your family sends in a month.

Social Studies Activity

Compare South America to another continent. How are they similar or different in size? How are they similar or different in the number of countries they contain?

Listening-and-Speaking Activity

Discuss with your family what you observed as your seeds grew during your science experiment. Explain your notes and your observations.

Directions: Read the text, and answer the questions on the next page.

The Not-So-Awful Bus Ride

Dylan was positive he was going to hate his new school in Seattle. He had discovered a decent skate park nearby, which was encouraging. But he didn't know anyone, so he was certain school would be horrible. On his first day, Dylan forced himself to get on the bus. He found a seat by himself and sat staring gloomily through the window. He ignored everyone else getting on the bus. He had already convinced himself that this was going to be a terrible day.

"You mind if I sit here?" asked a boy Dylan's age.

"Whatever," Dylan said.

"What's your name?" asked the boy.

"I'm Dylan." Then, after a pause, Dylan added, "What's yours?"

"Brad. I don't recognize you. Are you new?"

"Yeah," Dylan said. "We just moved to Seattle." Dylan wasn't sure what else to say. So he asked, "Do you play sports or anything?"

"Not that much," Brad responded. "Except for skateboarding."

"You skateboard?" Dylan asked, happily surprised.

"Yeah, I love it. Do you skateboard?" asked Brad.

"Whenever I can. There's a skate park near my house," said Dylan. Then, an idea occurred to him. Almost reluctantly, he said, "Maybe we could skate sometime."

"Yeah, that'd be great," agreed Brad. "We should."

Just then, the bus pulled into the parking lot. Everyone got off and headed to the building. Dylan had no idea where to go. When Brad noticed Dylan hesitating, he said, "I'm going by the office if you want to come along. They can tell you what your classes are."

"Yeah, okay," Dylan replied gratefully. Maybe this school wasn't going to be so terrible after all.

Reading

Directions: Read "The Not-So-Awful Bus Ride," and then answer the questions.

1. What would reading only the first sentence tell a reader about the text?
   - Ⓐ Dylan thinks he will not like his new school.
   - Ⓑ Dylan thinks he will have a good day at his new school.
   - Ⓒ Dylan thinks he will have an enjoyable bus ride.
   - Ⓓ Dylan thinks he will have an unpleasant bus ride.

2. A reader is most likely to read the text if he or she wants to
   - Ⓐ be persuaded to ride a bus.
   - Ⓑ be informed about public transportation.
   - Ⓒ be entertained by a fictional story.
   - Ⓓ learn how to drive a bus.

3. Why does Brad offer to show Dylan where the office is?
   - Ⓐ because Dylan is in trouble
   - Ⓑ because Dylan is sick
   - Ⓒ because Dylan is new and doesn't know where it is
   - Ⓓ because Brad doesn't want to go to school either

4. How does Dylan feel about going to school on the first day?
   - Ⓐ unhappy
   - Ⓑ excited
   - Ⓒ embarrassed
   - Ⓓ guilty

5. Who would best connect with the text?
   - Ⓐ a bus driver
   - Ⓑ a new student
   - Ⓒ a parent
   - Ⓓ a teacher

6. Which book title would you expect to share a theme similar to that of the text?
   - Ⓐ *Buddy the Bus*
   - Ⓑ *Bus Drivers of the World*
   - Ⓒ *My First Bus Buddy*
   - Ⓓ *Lonely at School*

Spelling

Directions: Write the plural of each word. Then, write two sentences using different plural words. Remember, when a noun ends in a vowel plus *–y*, add *–s*. When a noun ends in a consonant plus *–y*, change the *–y* to *–i* and add *–es*.

1. supply ____________________
2. blueberry ____________________
3. cavity ____________________
4. turkey ____________________
5. chimney ____________________
6. enemy ____________________
7. battery ____________________
8. mystery ____________________
9. pulley ____________________
10. journey ____________________

____

____

____

____

____

____

Directions: Circle the adjectives in the sentences.

1. We go on long drives during fall to see the leaves.
2. Finn likes sailing on beautiful Lake Louise.
3. However, you must use the black pits.
4. Elijah thinks decorative floats are the best part of the parade.
5. Bo is a huge sheepdog from Australia.
6. I want to go on fast roller coasters.
7. With this system, blind people could read.
8. Quails like to take dust baths.
9. The basketball was very slippery.
10. The fluffy kitten played with the red toy.

Writing

Directions: Imagine eating an ice cream cone. Brainstorm sensory details to describe the experience. Complete the graphic organizer with at least two details in each box.

Eating an Ice Cream Cone

See

Taste

Feel

Smell

Directions: Write a narrative about a time you were eating an ice cream cone. Include what the ice cream looked like and how it felt, tasted, and smelled. Use your notes on page 86 to help you.

Edit and Revise

A strong narrative paragraph:

- includes an introductory and a concluding sentence
- uses sensory details to describe the experience
- sounds like a story

Writing

Directions: Solve each problem.

❶ **Books Read in March**

Cathy	
Martin	
Jose	

= one book

Which children read the same number of books?

____

____

❷ **School Awards**

Students						
Daniel						
Evan						
Rich						

0 2 4 6 8 10 12

Number of Awards

How many awards did Daniel win?

____

❸ Record the data in the chart.

Child's Name	Number of Toys

- Jahir has 23 toys.
- Olivia has 15 toys.
- Gerald has 35 toys.
- Mimi has 3 toys.

❹ **Dollars Earned in May**

Audrey	$15
Dameon	$23
Jason	$12
Lauren	$18

What was the total amount of money earned in May by the children?

____

Directions: Solve each problem.

1 **Total Rainfall**

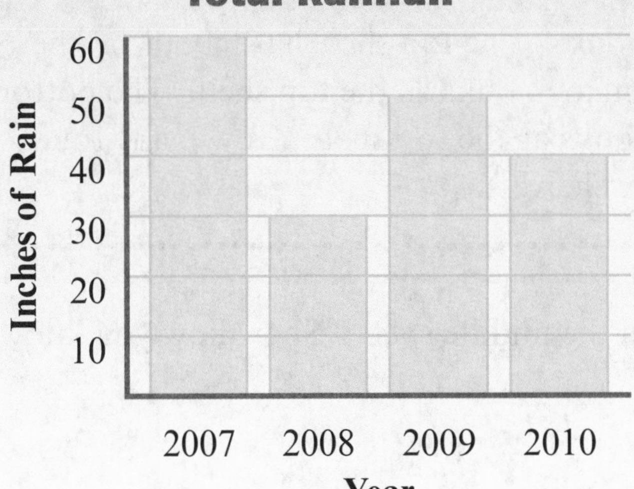

What was the total rainfall for all four years combined?

____

2 **Sports Played Each Year**

	Fall	Winter	Spring
Troy	soccer	basketball	basketball
Jessica	golf	basketball	track
Allison	soccer	diving	swimming

Who does not play basketball?

____

3 Record the data in the bar graph.

Home Runs Hit

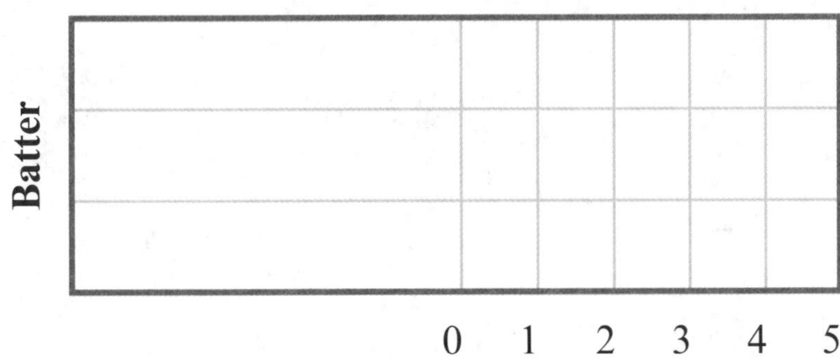

- Sara hit 4.
- Dean hit 5.
- Juan hit 2.

Problem Solving

Directions: Read and solve the problem.

There are three shelves of books. The top shelf has 6 books. The middle shelf has 9 times as many books as the top shelf. The bottom shelf has 7 times as many books as the top shelf. How many total books are on all three of the shelves?

1. How many books are on the middle shelf? Show how you know.

2. How many books are on the bottom shelf? Show how you know.

3. Choose a strategy to find the number of books on all three shelves. Show your work.

Directions: Read and solve the problem.

Mrs. Banks asks her students to write five multiplication equations with the product 1,200 and five division equations with the quotient 1,200.

1. List all of the factor pairs of 12.

____

____

2. How can the factor pairs of 12 help you write the multiplication equations?

____

____

3. How can you use multiplication to help you write the division equations?

____

____

____

4. Write five equations in each section of the table.

Multiplication Equations	Division Equations

Problem Solving

Social Studies

Directions: Goods are things that people buy and sell. Services are things that people do for money. Write 10 goods and 10 services in the chart. Circle the ones you use most often.

Goods	Services

Directions: Follow the steps in this experiment to discover how fossils are made.

What You Need

- pictures of fossils
- large bowl
- soil
- natural objects (no plastic or metal)
- wooden spoon
- water

What to Do

1. Look at the pictures of fossils. How do you think they were formed?

 ____

 ____

2. Make a model of an inland sea by placing soil in the bowl, adding water, and mixing it into mud.

3. Drop some natural objects into your inland sea.

4. Place the bowl in a sunny place for a few days to allow it to dry.

5. Break open your dried-out sea and examine the "fossils" you've made. Draw what you see.

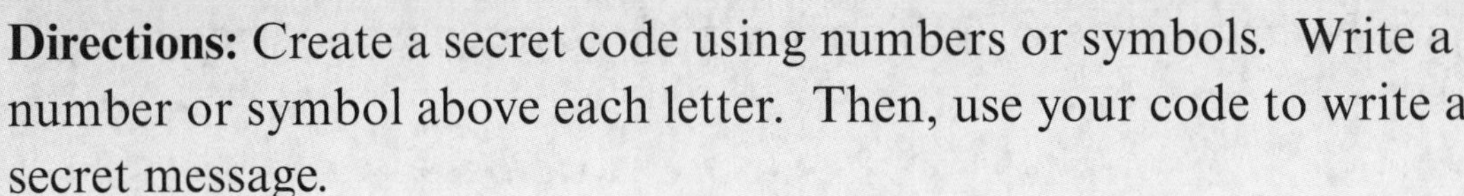

Directions: Create a secret code using numbers or symbols. Write a number or symbol above each letter. Then, use your code to write a secret message.

____	____	____	____	____	____
A	B	C	D	E	F
____	____	____	____	____	____
G	H	I	J	K	L
____	____	____	____	____	____
M	N	O	P	Q	R
____	____	____	____	____	____
S	T	U	V	W	X
		____	____		
		Y	Z		

____

____

____

Have a friend translate.

____

____

____

Directions: Play with three or more people. Begin by rolling a number cube. Match the roll to the category listed in the key. Give an example of something in that category. Then, the next player must also list something in that category without repeating. Continue until a player is not able to list something. Place a check mark next to that player's name. Then, the next person rolls, and the round starts over. If a person gets three check marks, he or she is out.

Game

Key	
1	Goods
2	Services
3	Needs
4	Wants
5	Expensive Items
6	Inexpensive Items

Player 1

____

Player 2

____

Player 3

____

Player 4

____

Spelling Activity

Practice your spelling words from page 84 by writing them in cursive with brightly colored markers. Write each word in a different color.

Writing Activity

An adjective such as *delicious* is not very specific. Adjectives such as *salty, sweet, creamy*, and *juicy* are much more specific. Revise your paragraph on page 87 to use more specific adjectives.

Mathematics Activity

Keep track of the high and low temperatures in your area over the course of a week. Then, make a line graph reflecting the data you collected.

Social Studies Activity

Add three more goods and three more services to the chart on page 92.

Science Activity

Use the library or the Internet to find out more about fossils. Where are they found? How old are they? Write a paragraph to summarize your findings.

Listening-and-Speaking Activity

After dinner, describe the food you ate using the most precise language that you can.

Directions: Read the text, and answer the questions on the next page.

Polygons Are Everywhere!

You already know a lot about shapes. You learn about shapes in your mathematics class. Maybe you have learned about polygons. Polygons are closed shapes. They have more than one side, and they have more than one angle. But polygons aren't just in your mathematics class. You can see polygons everywhere.

Most slices of pizza are triangles, and triangles are polygons. They are polygons because they have three sides and three angles.

A pentagon is a polygon that has five sides and five angles. There is a very big pentagon in Washington, DC. It's a building that has five sides and five angles, so it is called the Pentagon. The Pentagon is a very important place. The United States military leaders work in the Pentagon. They help keep the country safe. If you visit Washington, DC, maybe you can go to the Pentagon. If you do, you will be inside a polygon!

Hexagons are also polygons. Hexagons have six sides and six angles. Where can you find a hexagon? Just look for bees! When bees make honey, they store it in honeycombs. Each cell of a honeycomb is a hexagon. If you see a honeycomb, you will see hexagons. But be careful of the bees!

How many sides does an octagon have? An octagon has eight sides and eight angles. You can tell because the word starts with the prefix *oct–*, which means *eight*. Octagons have more than one side and more than one angle, so they are polygons. You see octagons every time you see a stop sign! Stop signs have eight sides and eight angles. That makes them octagons.

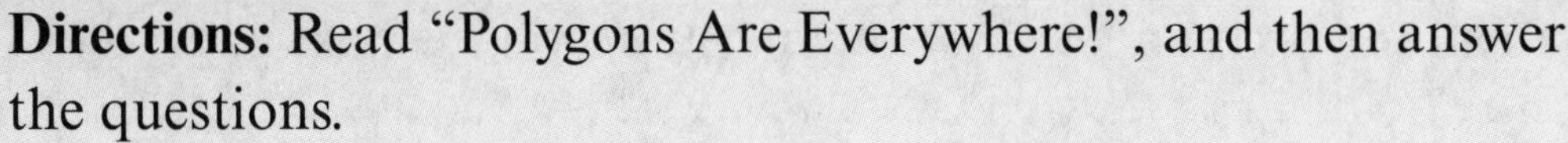

Directions: Read "Polygons Are Everywhere!", and then answer the questions.

Reading

1. Which of these would not be a good alternative title for the text?
   - (A) "Polygons All Around Us"
   - (B) "My Favorite Pizza"
   - (C) "Polygons and Prefixes"
   - (D) "Where to Find Polygons"

2. A reader would most likely read the text to be
   - (A) persuaded to do something.
   - (B) entertained by a fictional story.
   - (C) instructed how to make a pizza.
   - (D) informed about everyday shapes.

3. Which polygon is NOT defined in the text?
   - (A) octagon
   - (B) hexagon
   - (C) pentagon
   - (D) nonagon

4. Which is NOT true about polygons?
   - (A) They are closed shapes.
   - (B) They have more than one side.
   - (C) They are hard to find.
   - (D) They have more than one angle.

5. People who like ______ will probably like this text.
   - (A) music
   - (B) art
   - (C) mathematics
   - (D) sports

6. Which statement is true?
   - (A) A triangle is not a polygon.
   - (B) Honeycombs are octagons.
   - (C) You can see polygons in many places.
   - (D) The Pentagon has six sides and six angles.

Directions: Write each word. Then, write each word backward.

1. slay ______________ ______________
2. stray ______________ ______________
3. holiday ______________ ______________
4. Monday ______________ ______________
5. stain ______________ ______________
6. faith ______________ ______________
7. sprain ______________ ______________
8. plain ______________ ______________
9. aim ______________ ______________
10. afraid ______________ ______________

Spelling

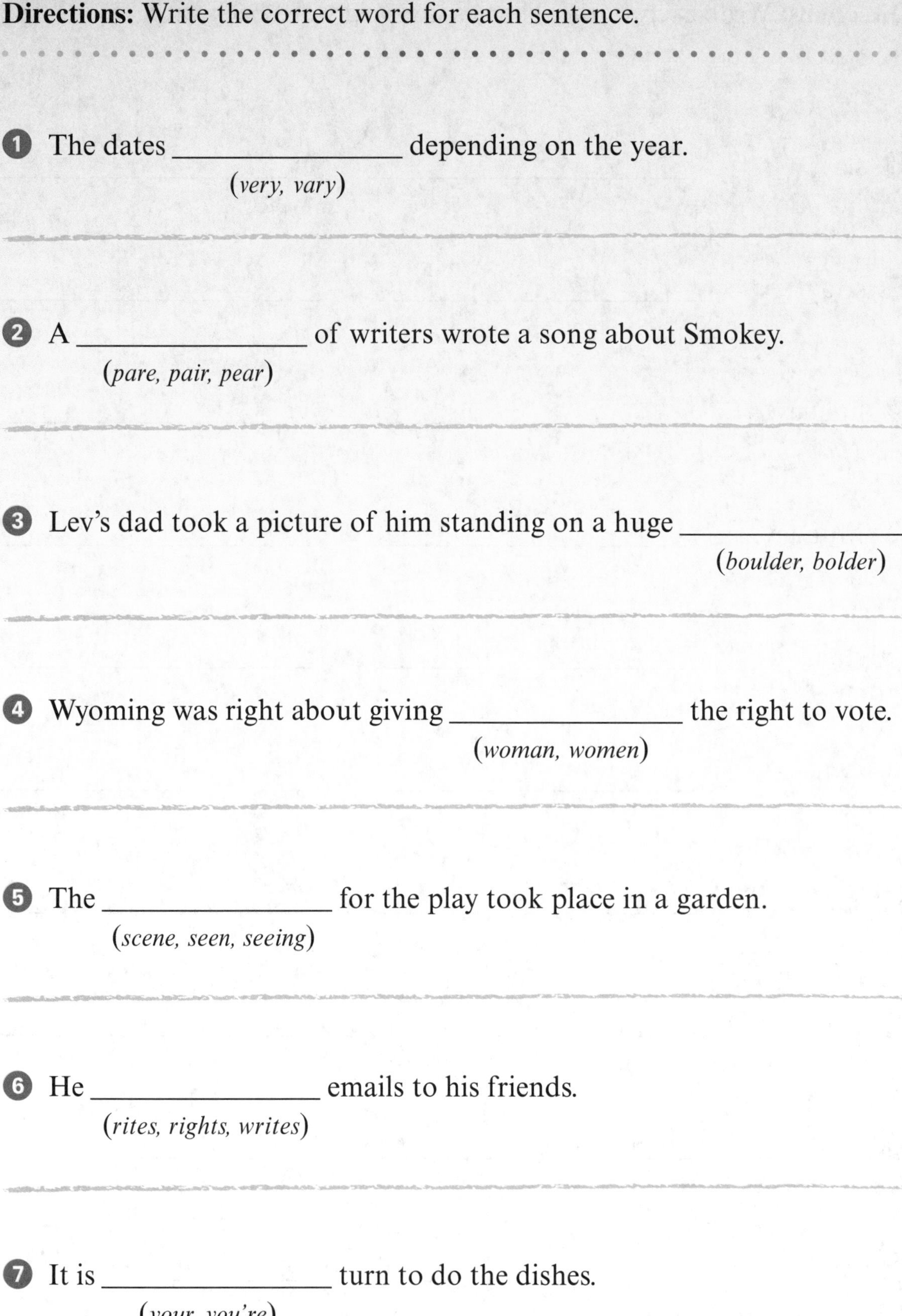

Directions: Write the correct word for each sentence.

1. The dates _______________ depending on the year.
   (*very, vary*)

2. A _______________ of writers wrote a song about Smokey.
   (*pare, pair, pear*)

3. Lev's dad took a picture of him standing on a huge _______________.
   (*boulder, bolder*)

4. Wyoming was right about giving _______________ the right to vote.
   (*woman, women*)

5. The _______________ for the play took place in a garden.
   (*scene, seen, seeing*)

6. He _______________ emails to his friends.
   (*rites, rights, writes*)

7. It is _______________ turn to do the dishes.
   (*your, you're*)

Language

Directions: Turbines can harness the wind's energy. Read the notes about using turbines. Decide if each note is an advantage or a disadvantage, and write it in the table below.

- no wind, no energy
- tall, but do not take up much land
- noisy to nearby homes and businesses
- birds killed by turbine blades
- wind is free
- does not create pollution or greenhouse gases
- clutter land, which some people say is ugly
- good for remote areas without access to electricity

Advantages	Disadvantages

Writing

Directions: Do you think turbines should be used to collect wind energy? Write your opinion and why you feel the way you do. Use the table from page 151 to help you write your opinion paragraph.

Edit and Revise

A strong opinion paragraph includes:

- an introductory sentence that states your opinion
- details to support your ideas
- a concluding sentence

Directions: Solve each problem.

1. Draw at least one line of symmetry.

2. How many lines of symmetry does a pentagon have?

____

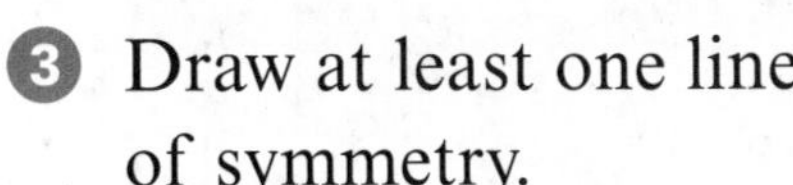

3. Draw at least one line of symmetry.

4. Draw at least one line of symmetry.

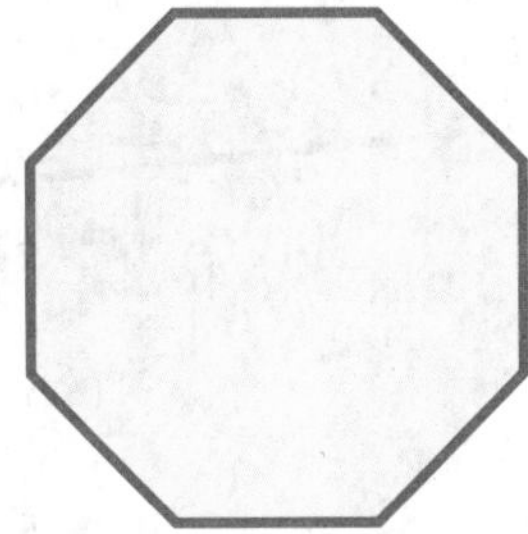

5. Name the shape of the solid's base.

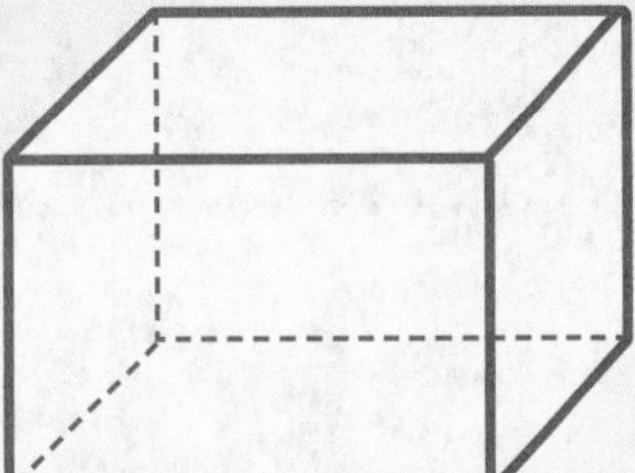

____

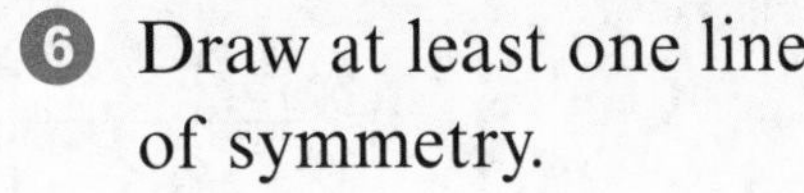

6. Draw at least one line of symmetry.

7. Name this shape.

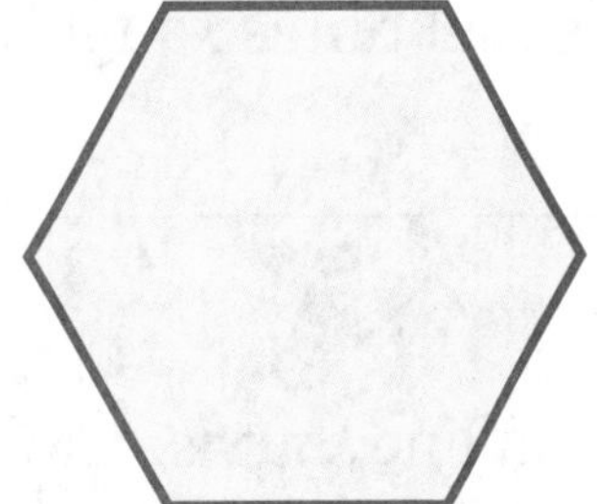

____

Mathematics

Directions: Solve each problem.

1. I have one curved surface, no edges, and no corners. What solid am I?

____

2. I have two circular bases and my other face is curved. What solid am I?

____

3. An equilateral triangle has:

_______ angles _______ sides _______ axes of symmetry

4. Do parallel or perpendicular lines meet at right angles?

____

5. A rectangle has:

_______ angles _______ sides _______ axes of symmetry

6. Name a two-dimensional shape that has two equal acute angles and two equal obtuse angles.

____

7. Draw a line that is parallel to the line below.

Problem Solving

Directions: Read and solve the problem.

Jermaine is thinking of a shape that has exactly one set of parallel sides and at least two right angles.

1. How many sides must the shape have?

____

2. Draw the shape. Label the parallel sides and the right angles.

3. What type of polygon did you draw? Is there another type of polygon you can draw to match this description? Explain your thinking.

____

____

____

____

____

____

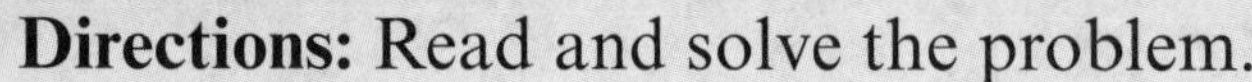

Directions: Read and solve the problem.

Problem Solving

Gloria is making a necklace with beads in the shapes of stars, suns, and moons. She begins by placing one sun, two moons, and two stars on the necklace. If she continues this pattern, what will be the 100th bead on the necklace?

1. Sketch the first ten beads in the necklace.

2. How can your sketch help you determine the 100th bead? Solve the problem, and justify your solution.

3. Using the star, sun, and moon beads, draw a necklace pattern of your own. Determine what the 100th bead on your necklace will be.

Directions: In the 1800s, Americans began moving west. Before the end of the century, they had spread all the way to the Pacific Ocean. Research westward expansion during that time. Then, answer the questions.

1. Why did people want to move west in the 1800s?

   ____

   ____

   ____

2. Describe the journeys of pioneers moving west.

   ____

   ____

   ____

   ____

3. What was life like for pioneers once they reached the frontier?

   ____

   ____

   ____

   ____

4. How did westward expansion affect American Indian tribes?

   ____

   ____

   ____

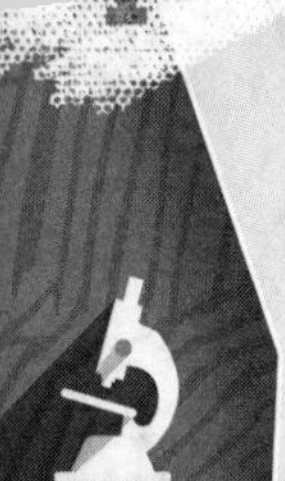

Science

Directions: Follow the steps in this experiment to discover what happens to chalk in vinegar.

What You Need

- three clear plastic cups
- three pieces of chalk
- lemon juice
- vinegar
- water

What to Do

1. Fill each cup halfway—one with lemon juice, one with vinegar, and one with water.
2. Place one piece of chalk in each cup. Leave the cups in a safe place.
3. Make a prediction. What will happen in the different cups?

____

____

4. Observe the cups each day for three days. Draw and label diagrams to record what you see.

Directions: Look at the photo for 30 seconds. Then, cover it up, and list as many things as you can remember.

- ____
- ____
- ____
- ____
- ____
- ____
- ____
- ____
- ____
- ____

Directions: Work with a partner. Use small objects to mark your spots on the game board. Take turns rolling a number cube. Move the number of spaces that you roll. If you land on a space with words, draw that shape on a sheet of paper. Add one line of symmetry to your shape. Some spaces let you create your own shape. Just remember, it needs at least one line of symmetry. The first person to reach the finish line wins.

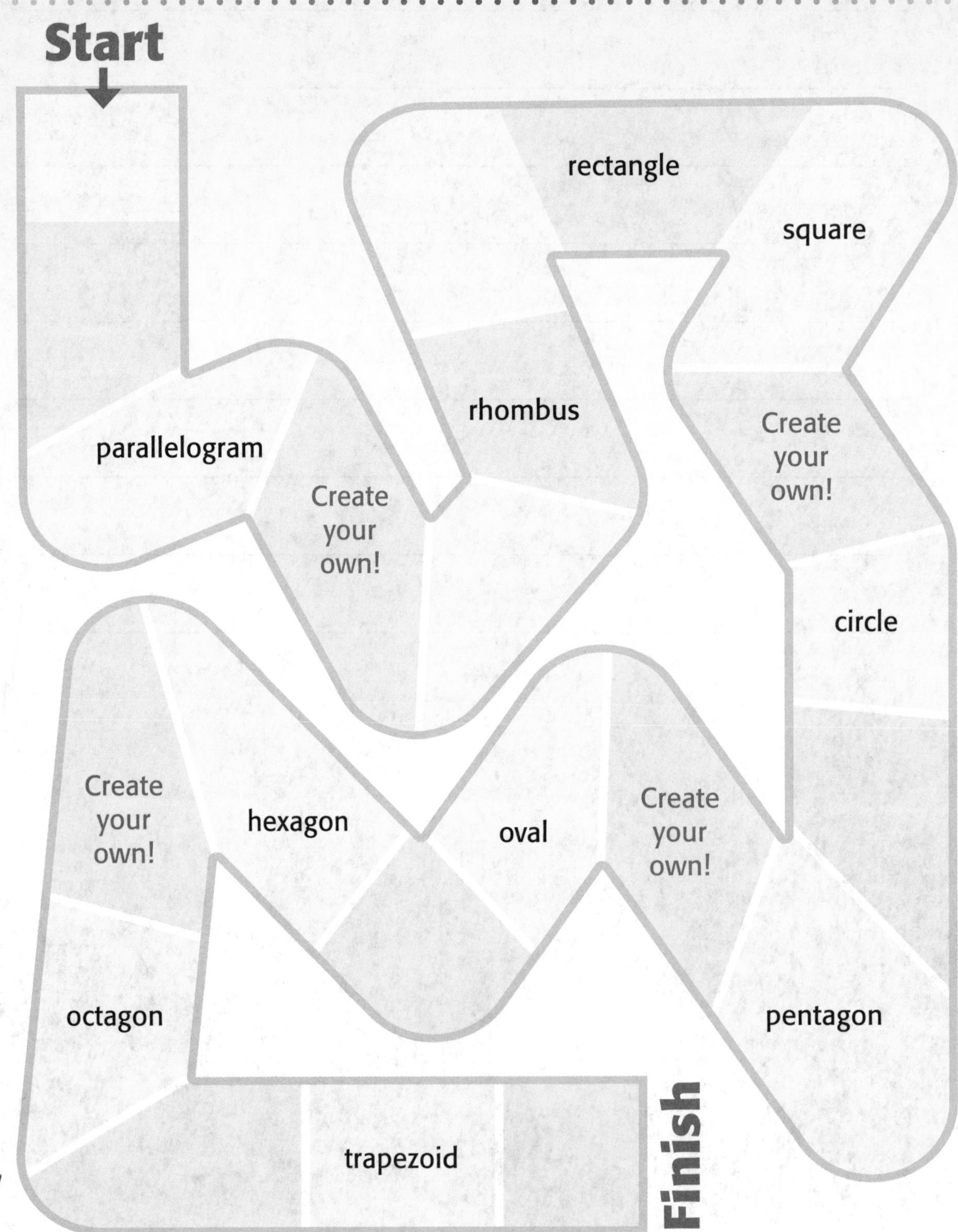

Spelling Activity

Write silly sentences with the spelling words on page 99 in your best cursive handwriting.

Writing Activity

Reread your paragraph on page 102. Underline your opinion statement in red. Underline your supporting details in green. Underline your concluding statement in blue. Make revisions as needed.

Mathematics Activity

Look through a magazine, and select a picture of an object. Position a small mirror on the picture to create symmetry. Half of the object will be from the picture, and half will be reflected in the mirror.

Problem-Solving Activity

Create a pattern using small objects. Determine what the 20th item in your pattern will be. Then, create a new pattern using the same objects. Determine what the 50th item in your new pattern will be.

Science Activity

Research acid rain in the library or on the Internet. How is it similar to the experiment on page 108? How is it different?

Listening-and-Speaking Activity

Tell your family what you learned about westward expansion. Explain the experiences of pioneers and American Indians in the 1800s.

Reading

Directions: Read the text, and answer the questions on the next page.

Time to Get Organized!

Grace knew she needed to talk to her teacher, Mrs. Wilson. She was having trouble in class, and it was mostly because she kept forgetting things. After class, Grace waited until everyone had left and then approached Mrs. Wilson's desk.

"I know I did really badly on the exam today," Grace began. "I could have done a whole lot better."

"What do you think happened?" Mrs. Wilson asked. She wanted to get Grace's point of view.

"I think it's because I keep forgetting things. I forgot we were having an exam today, so I didn't think about studying like I usually do. That happens to me a lot because I do a lot of activities. Keeping everything organized is really hard for me."

"What other things do you do?" Mrs. Wilson wanted to know.

"Well, there's school, and I take piano lessons. I also write articles for the school newspaper. And I want to have fun with my friends."

"It sounds like you're busy, but that doesn't mean you can't get organized. You need to manage your time better," Mrs. Wilson said.

"That's what my parents tell me, too," Grace said with a sigh.

"Well, they're right," Mrs. Wilson said. "And you can begin getting organized by getting a calendar. If you get a large calendar, you can write everything you need to do. Then, every day, you can check your calendar to see what's on your schedule."

Grace was beginning to get the idea. "And I can write my assignments and tests on my calendar, too, so I don't forget to study!"

"Exactly!" Mrs. Wilson said. "If you know you have an exam in a week, you can begin studying a little every day. That way, you'll be prepared for the exam, but you'll still have time for other things."

Directions: Read "Time to Get Organized!", and then answer the questions.

1. After reading this text, a reader will be able to
   - (A) explain why organization is important.
   - (B) explain what a calendar is.
   - (C) talk about classrooms.
   - (D) warn students about how hard exams are.

2. The author most likely wrote this to
   - (A) entertain readers so that they will want to read more.
   - (B) inform readers on proper classroom behavior.
   - (C) persuade readers to learn about calendars.
   - (D) persuade readers to become organized.

3. What might happen if Grace gets a calendar?
   - (A) Grace will do poorly on all her tests.
   - (B) Grace will not forget to do things.
   - (C) Grace's parents will be angry with her.
   - (D) Mrs. Wilson will get Grace a calendar.

4. If Grace studies a little every day, she will
   - (A) forget everything.
   - (B) be ready for the exam and still have time for other things.
   - (C) take piano lessons and practice piano every day.
   - (D) write everything on her calendar.

5. Which would best help Grace become organized?
   - (A) a computer with a digital calendar
   - (B) a computer for playing video games
   - (C) talking to Mrs. Wilson each night about homework
   - (D) none of the above

6. Grace is most similar to the hare in "The Tortoise and the Hare" because
   - (A) she knows what to do.
   - (B) she is slow but always finishes.
   - (C) she is disorganized but very quick.
   - (D) her lack of planning causes her to do poorly.

Spelling

Directions: Write each word in printing and in cursive.

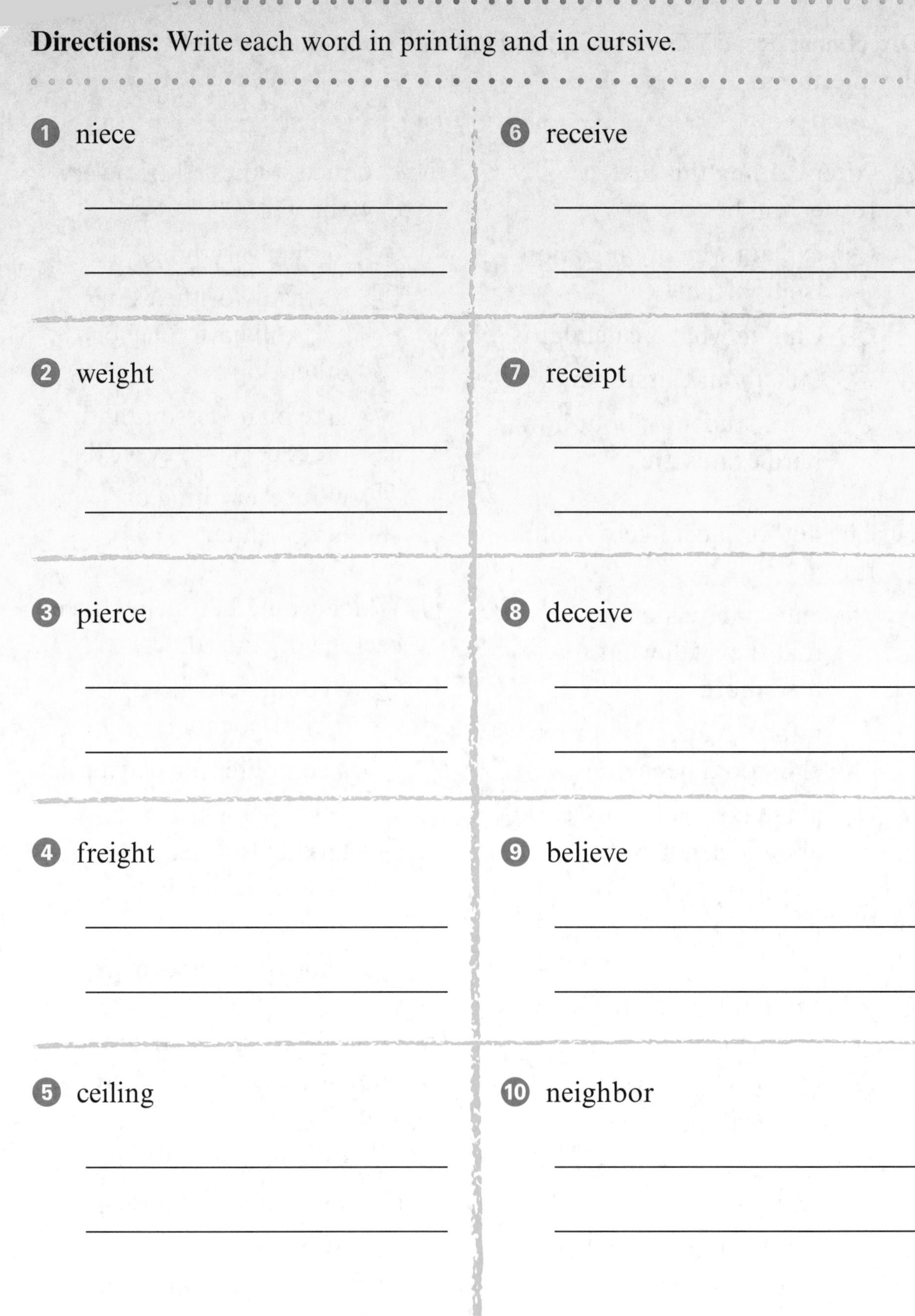

1. niece
6. receive
2. weight
7. receipt
3. pierce
8. deceive
4. freight
9. believe
5. ceiling
10. neighbor

Directions: Circle the prepositional phrases in the sentences.

1. Gus likes vanilla ice cream on a cone.
2. His shoes were on the wrong feet.
3. The elephant was 11 feet tall at the shoulders.
4. The hardest thing to find on the list was a broken skate.
5. Alexander was rescued after nearly five years.
6. The kids shout loudly in the rink.
7. The cat is black except for three white paws.
8. Some pigs are trained to perform in a show.
9. A happy girl ran down the street.
10. In the basement, they found a dusty suitcase.

Writing

Directions: This web is about Henry Ford's early car, the Model-T. Place check marks in the parts of the web that should be included in an informative/explanatory paragraph about the production of the Model-T.

Production of the Model-T

- It was made with interchangeable parts, so the car took less time to make.
- Workers were paid $5.00 a day; most other workers were paid $2.34 a day.
- It was made on a moving assembly line, so the car was less expensive to make.
- It was nicknamed the "Tin Lizzie."
- I like the way the Model-T looks.
- I have seen a Model-T in a museum.
- It was introduced in October 1908.

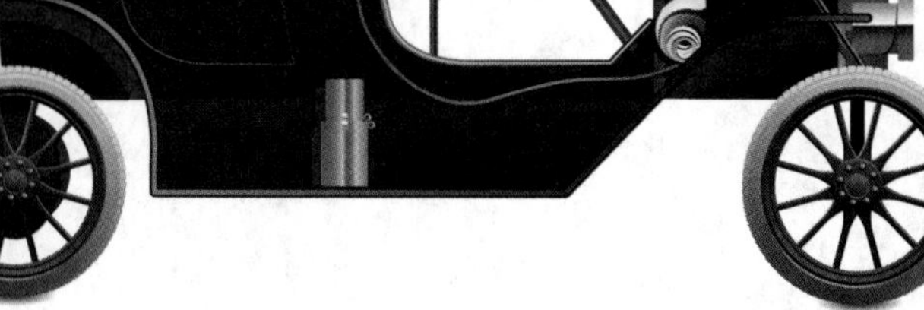

Directions: Write an informative/explanatory paragraph about the production of Henry Ford's Model-T car. Include facts about the Model-T and the employees who helped make the cars. Use the information on page 116 to help you.

Edit and Revise!

A strong informative/explanatory paragraph includes:

- introductory and concluding sentences
- details which support the main idea

Writing

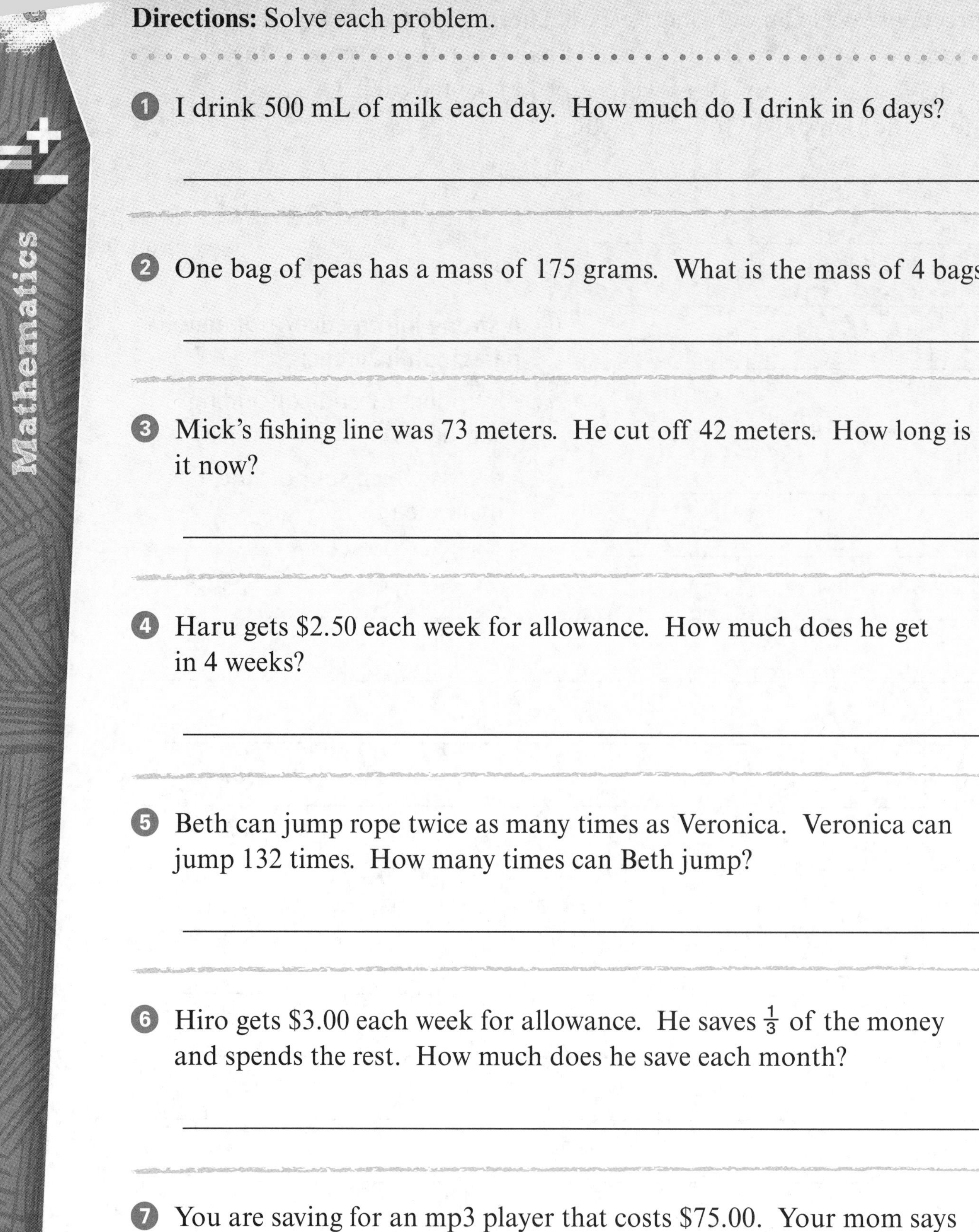

Directions: Solve each problem.

1. I drink 500 mL of milk each day. How much do I drink in 6 days?

2. One bag of peas has a mass of 175 grams. What is the mass of 4 bags?

3. Mick's fishing line was 73 meters. He cut off 42 meters. How long is it now?

4. Haru gets $2.50 each week for allowance. How much does he get in 4 weeks?

5. Beth can jump rope twice as many times as Veronica. Veronica can jump 132 times. How many times can Beth jump?

6. Hiro gets $3.00 each week for allowance. He saves $\frac{1}{3}$ of the money and spends the rest. How much does he save each month?

7. You are saving for an mp3 player that costs $75.00. Your mom says she will help you by paying for $\frac{1}{3}$ of the cost. How much do you still have to save?

Directions: Solve each problem.

1. Is 0.6 greater than 0.59?

2. Half of 30 is

3. Is 0.7 less than 0.59?

4. Half of 60 is

5. Write $\frac{73}{100}$ as a decimal.

6. Write $\frac{37}{100}$ as a decimal.

7. Write 0.35 as a fraction.

8. Write 0.2 as a fraction.

9. Write 0.45 as a fraction.

10. What is $\frac{1}{3}$ of 18?

Mathematics

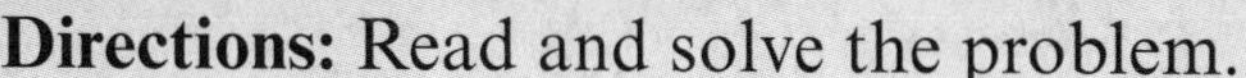

Problem Solving

Directions: Read and solve the problem.

Sarah has a bag of 57 lollipops. She sorts them into equal groups to give away to her friends. She saves 3 leftover lollipops for herself. Write three different division equations that show how Sarah can sort the lollipops into equal groups and have 3 remaining for herself.

1. In your division equation, what will the quotient represent?

____

____

2. In your division equation, what will the factor dividing 57 represent?

____

____

3. Write and solve three division equations.

Directions: Read and solve the problem.

There are 20 adult chaperones and 64 students attending an outdoor field trip. The principal wants each chaperone on the trip to have 4 bottles of water and each student to have 3 bottles of water. How many packages of water must the school purchase if the bottles of water come in packages of 8?

1. How many bottles of water will be needed for the adult chaperones?

2. How many bottles of water will be needed for the students?

3. Choose a strategy to show how many packages of water must be purchased.

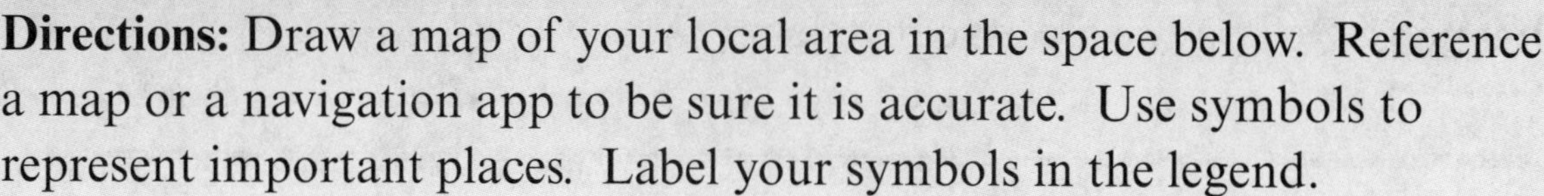
Directions: Draw a map of your local area in the space below. Reference a map or a navigation app to be sure it is accurate. Use symbols to represent important places. Label your symbols in the legend.

Social Studies

Legend

Directions: Follow the steps in this experiment to discover how digestion works.

What You Need

- two plastic zipper bags
- lemon juice
- water
- teaspoon
- one crushed cookie

What to Do

1. Place 5 mL (1 tsp) of crushed cookie into a plastic zipper bag. Add enough water to just cover the cookie. This is your control.
2. Place 5 mL (1 tsp) of crushed cookie into the other bag. Add enough lemon juice to just cover the cookie.
3. Leave both bags overnight.
4. The next day, observe the crushed cookie in each bag. Tip some of the mixture out so that you can feel it with your fingertips. Describe what you see, feel, and smell.

Water: ____

____

____

____

Lemon Juice: ____

____

____

____

Critical Thinking

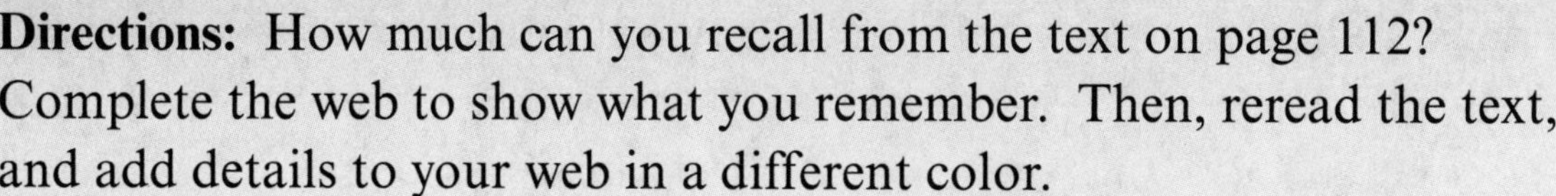

Directions: How much can you recall from the text on page 112? Complete the web to show what you remember. Then, reread the text, and add details to your web in a different color.

"Time to Get Organized"

Who

What

Where

When

Directions: Play with a partner. Place a paper clip in the center of the circle, and place the point of a pencil through the paper clip. This will be your spinner. For each turn, flick your paper clip to spin. Write the amount you spin in the chart. After each player has had eight turns, add up your scores. The person with the highest score wins.

$0.25

$0.66 **$0.76**

$0.22 **$1.25**

$5.47 **$2.43**

$3.38 **$6.04**

$8.32

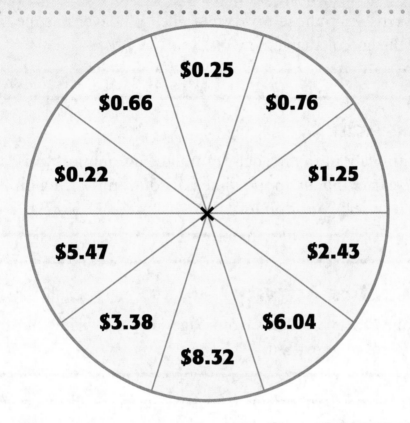

Player 1	Player 2

Spelling Activity

Write each word from page 114 on two squares of paper. Mix up the words, and turn them face down. Play a memory game with a partner. Take turns trying to match up the words. If you match a pair of words, keep those words in a pile. Whoever has the most words at the end of the game wins.

Writing Activity

After writing about the Model-T, think of an opinion you have about the car. Find an appropriate part of your writing on page 117 in which to insert your opinion.

Mathematics Activity

Choose one of the problems from page 119, and write your own story problem to go with it.

Social Studies Activity

Use the map you created on page 122 to write directions to three different places.

Science Activity

Research the digestive system. How does the stomach relate to the experiment on page 123?

Listening-and-Speaking Activity

Read your paragraph from page 117 aloud to a family member. Be sure to use appropriate expression.

Directions: Read the text, and answer the questions on the next page.

Reading

Welcome Aboard!

Welcome aboard! You are going on a cruise! A cruise is a special kind of vacation on a very large ship. Cruise ships travel to many different places. When you take a cruise, you sleep in a room called a cabin. Cabins aren't very big, but they have beds, bathrooms, and televisions. However, most people don't spend very much time in their cabins because there are so many fun activities to do on a cruise.

Different cruises last for various amounts of time. Some cruises last four days, and others last as long as two weeks. During the cruise, the ship makes stops in different cities, islands, or national parks. You can get off the ship and visit those places while the ship is there. While you are visiting, you can swim, hike, or explore. You can shop, take a walk, try a new activity, or just sit and relax. Then, it's time to get back on board the ship so that it can go to the next place on your cruise. But don't worry—there is so much you can do on a cruise ship that you won't get bored.

Most cruise ships have swimming pools, so you can go swimming on board the ship. Many cruise ships have exciting games and fun contests you can enter. They also have plays, shows, and places to shop. Some offer miniature golf, tennis, and even rock climbing! You never get hungry on a cruise, either. Cruise ships have several restaurants and other places to eat. No matter what kind of food you enjoy, you'll find it on a cruise ship.

Many people work on the cruise ship to help keep you safe and be sure you have a good vacation. The captain is in charge of the ship. The cruise director is the person who organizes the activities. There are many other crew members, too. All of them are there to answer questions, make sure the ship is safe, and make sure you enjoy yourself.

Reading

Directions: Read "Welcome Aboard!", and then answer the questions.

1. Does the title provide enough information to make a prediction about the text?
   - (A) Yes. It tells the reader that the text is about being aboard a train.
   - (B) Yes. It tells the reader that the text is about being aboard cruise ships.
   - (C) No. The text could be about being aboard a train, a ship, or an airplane.
   - (D) No. The text could be about being bored in the car.

2. A reader would most likely read the text to
   - (A) find out what a cruise is like.
   - (B) learn how to play tennis.
   - (C) find out where to go swimming.
   - (D) learn how to become a captain.

3. Which is NOT something people can do on a cruise ship?
   - (A) shop
   - (B) play tennis
   - (C) swim
   - (D) hike

4. Which sentence is true?
   - (A) All cruises last for one week.
   - (B) Most cruises have one restaurant.
   - (C) Cruises have many games, shows, and activities.
   - (D) The cruise director is in charge of the cruise ship.

5. People who like to ______ will probably enjoy a cruise.
   - (A) be alone
   - (B) rest
   - (C) try new activities
   - (D) play video games

6. Most people do not spend much time in their ______ even though they sleep in them.
   - (A) hotel rooms
   - (B) bedrooms
   - (C) cabins
   - (D) bedchambers

Directions: Write your own definition of each word. Use a dictionary if you don't know its meaning. Then, cover the word, and write it in the box.

1. comfortable
2. lovable
3. noticeable
4. agreeable
5. affordable
6. possible
7. visible
8. terrible

Spelling

Language

Directions: Circle the articles in the sentences.

1. In 1962, the Chicago River was green for a week after St. Patrick's Day.
2. Some people think the fables came from many storytellers.
3. At first, the games in the Olympics were all races.
4. Franklin learned later that he paid too much for the whistle.
5. Mai had read about a female pirate named Anne Bonny.
6. The spacecraft searched for signs of life.
7. The National Baseball Hall of Fame is in New York.
8. A piano company called Steinway & Sons makes more than 2,000 pianos each year.
9. Saad wanted to read a book.
10. My mom likes to wash the car every week.

Directions: Use the flowchart to write ideas for a narrative paragraph about a fourth grader going ice skating for the first time. You can use your imagination or your own experiences.

Beginning

Middle

End

Directions: Write a narrative about a fourth grader going ice skating for the first time. Include details of the experience and how the character felt. Use your notes from page 131 to help you.

Writing

Edit and Revise

A strong narrative paragraph:

- has a beginning, a middle, and an end
- tells events in order
- uses dialogue and descriptions

Directions: Solve each problem.

1. List all the factors of 6.

2. List all the factors of 4.

3. List all the factors of 9.

4. List all the factors of 16.

5. List all the factors of 18.

6. List all the factors of 8.

7. List all the factors of 24.

8. List all the factors of 20.

9. List all the factors of 25.

Mathematics

Mathematics

Directions: Solve each problem.

1. List all the factors of 36.

   ____

2. List all the factors of 30.

   ____

3. Complete the chart with the missing factors. One has been done for you.

product	24	25	28	30
factor	3	5	4	10
factor	8			

4. Complete the chart with the missing factors.

product	32	36	40	42
factor	4	6	5	6
factor				

5. Complete the chart with the missing factors.

product	48	56	60	81
factor	8	7	6	9
factor				

6. List the first 3 multiples of 7.

   __________ __________ __________

Directions: Read and solve the problem.

Derrick plays baseball and soccer. The calendar shows the days he has practice.

B—Baseball practice **S**—Soccer practice

Sunday	Monday	Tuesday	Wednesday	Thursday	Friday	Saturday
B	X	S	S	B	X	S
S	B	X	S	S	B	S

1. Complete each statement:

- Derrick practices ______________________ $\frac{1}{2}$ of the time.
- Derrick practices ______________________ $\frac{2}{7}$ of the time.
- Derrick has an off-day $\frac{\square}{14}$ of the time.

2. After the schedule above is completed, soccer season ends. Soccer practice days will become off-days. Baseball practice days remain the same. Complete this calendar, showing Derrick's new schedule.

Sunday	Monday	Tuesday	Wednesday	Thursday	Friday	Saturday

3. Write three equivalent fractions representing Derrick's off-days on his new schedule.

____

Problem Solving

Directions: Read and solve the problem.

A family orders three equal-sized small pizzas for dinner. The pepperoni pizza is cut into 8 slices, the cheese pizza is cut into 4 slices, and the vegetable pizza is cut into 6 slices. The family eats 5 slices of the pepperoni pizza, 2 slices of the cheese pizza, and 2 slices of the vegetable pizza.

1. Show the amount of each pizza the family eats. Shade and label each model.

_______________ _______________ _______________

2. Use your models to write what fraction of each pizza is left over.

____

____

____

3. Choose a strategy to list the fractional amounts of leftover pizza in order from least to greatest. Justify your solution.

____

____

____

Directions: Answer the questions.

1. List three leaders that you know.

2. What qualities make someone a good leader? Why are these qualities important?

3. Do you think you are a good leader? Explain.

4. How can you be a leader at home and in the community?

Social Studies

Directions: Follow the steps in this experiment to discover how fast cloth dries.

What You Need

- three identical pieces of cloth
- water
- string
- pegs

Science

What to Do

1. Dip the three pieces of cloth in water. Then, squeeze out as much water as you can.

2. Choose places to hang the cloths with the string and pegs. Put one somewhere you think it will dry quickly and one somewhere you think it will dry slowly. Keep one cloth separate as a control.

3. Check the cloths every ten minutes. Record how long it takes each cloth to dry.

   - I put the first cloth ______________________ to dry quickly.
   - It took ______________________ to dry.
   - I put the second cloth ______________________ to dry slowly.
   - It took ______________________ to dry.
   - I put the last cloth ______________________ as a control.
   - It took ______________________ to dry.

4. Why do you think some cloths dry slower or faster?

____

____

____

Directions: Look at each set of words or numbers. Sort the words or numbers into two categories. Label the categories on each chart. Then, explain why you sorted them that way.

- orange
- potato
- grapefruit
- garlic
- pineapple
- lettuce
- zucchini
- tomato

Category:	**Category:**

Why did you sort the words this way?

____

____

16	91	27	610	88
63	255	17	72	25

Category:	**Category:**

Why did you sort the numbers this way?

____

____

Directions: Play with a partner. Take turns rolling two number cubes. Use the key to match your roll to the corresponding word. Roll again to find a second word. Write a sentence using both words. If you roll a 12, choose a word that is not in the key. After you have each written three sentences, work together to create a story using as many of your sentences as you can.

Key			
2	comfortable	**7**	possible
3	lovable	**8**	visible
4	noticeable	**9**	terrible
5	agreeable	**10**	edible
6	affordable	**11**	incredible

Player 1

1. ______________________
____
____

2. ______________________
____
____

3. ______________________
____
____

Player 2

1. ______________________
____
____

2. ______________________
____
____

3. ______________________
____
____

Spelling Activity

Review the words on page 129. Think of three more words that end in *–able* or *–ible*. Write a sentence using each one.

Writing Activity

Draw a box around each section of your story from page 132 (beginning, middle, end). Check that the ideas flow smoothly from one section to the next. Revise as needed.

Mathematics Activity

As quickly as you can, write the factors of all even numbers between 2 and 20.

Social Studies Activity

Write a letter to a leader you know. Explain why he or she is a good leader.

Critical-Thinking Activity

Sort the words and numbers on page 139 a second time. How many other ways could you sort them?

Listening-and-Speaking Activity

Discuss leadership with your family. Ask them what qualities they think a good leader should have.

Reading

Directions: Read the text, and answer the questions on the next page.

A Very Wet Picnic

One Saturday, Tricia and her friend, Lisa, went to their favorite place. It was a creek that Tricia had found. Both girls had a backpack full of supplies. They had planned a picnic, and they had each brought food. Apart from food, Tricia brought a camera and a large bottle of water. Lisa brought water, a pad of paper, and some pens.

The girls arrived at the creek. Tricia pulled a soft, blue blanket out of her backpack and then took out some sandwiches and two green apples. Lisa opened her backpack and retrieved a banana and a few cookies. For a while, the two girls ate and drank without conversing much. When they finished, Tricia said, "Let's take some pictures." Lisa agreed, and they walked up and down the creek. They took pictures of what they saw. They took pictures of frogs and turtles. They took a picture of a salamander, the colorful leaves, and the countless flowers that surrounded them.

Then, Tricia and Lisa decided to draw their surroundings. They drew pictures of what they saw. They drew trees, rocks, the water, and some of the animals. All of a sudden, Lisa saw a drop fall on her paper. Then, she saw another drop, and more drops followed.

"It's starting to rain, Tricia," Lisa said in a panicked voice.

"Okay, let's pack up," Tricia answered. The two girls quickly put everything in their backpacks. Now, the rain was coming down harder. They were going to have to hurry home. They shrugged their backpacks on and sprinted as fast as they could back to Tricia's house. By that time, the storm had worsened. Rain lashed at the windows, and thunder boomed in the distance. When they arrived at Tricia's house, they raced inside, dripping water as they went.

Tricia's mother got the two girls some dry towels and helped them with their backpacks.

"At least we took pictures of our picnic before the rain really started to pour!" Lisa said thankfully.

Directions: Read "A Very Wet Picnic," and then answer the questions.

1. What happens as the girls are drawing?
   - Ⓐ It starts to rain.
   - Ⓑ Lisa's drink spills.
   - Ⓒ A salamander approaches them.
   - Ⓓ They decide to take pictures.

2. The purpose of this text is
   - Ⓐ to read about rain and wet grass.
   - Ⓑ to read about what a picnic is.
   - Ⓒ to read a story from the perspective of one character.
   - Ⓓ to read a story from the perspective of two characters.

3. What might happen next?
   - Ⓐ Lisa and Tricia will go to the creek.
   - Ⓑ Lisa and Tricia will dry off with the towels.
   - Ⓒ Lisa and Tricia will eat lunch.
   - Ⓓ Lisa and Tricia will draw a tree.

4. Why do you think Tricia and Lisa ran as fast as they could?
   - Ⓐ They are late for dinner.
   - Ⓑ They are afraid of the dark.
   - Ⓒ They saw something very scary at the creek.
   - Ⓓ They wanted to get out of the rain.

5. Tricia and Lisa resolve the rain issue by
   - Ⓐ packing up their picnic to keep things dry.
   - Ⓑ sprinting to Tricia's house.
   - Ⓒ taking shelter inside.
   - Ⓓ all of the above

6. This story is an example of
   - Ⓐ characters goofing around without planning anything out.
   - Ⓑ characters making plans and keeping them without any changes.
   - Ⓒ characters making plans but having to change them.
   - Ⓓ none of the above

Spelling

Directions: Write the contraction for each set of words. Write five more contractions you know in the chart.

1. you would ____________
2. they will ____________
3. would have ____________
4. should not ____________
5. I am ____________
6. he will ____________
7. they would ____________
8. could have ____________
9. I would ____________
10. we have ____________

Original Words	Contractions

Directions: Circle the correctly spelled word in each set.

1	affurd	aford	afford
2	except	exsept	eccept
3	buseist	busiest	bisiest
4	probubly	prabably	probably
5	portion	porton	porchun
6	folish	foolish	foulish
7	dangerous	dangerus	dangirous
8	favorite	favorete	favurite
9	believe	beleive	beleave

Directions: Read each fact about bullet trains. Decide whether you think each one is an advantage or a disadvantage, and place a check mark in that column. Then, write why you think the fact is an advantage or a disadvantage.

Fact	Advantage	Disadvantage	Why?
There are over 15 countries with bullet trains.			
Americans tend to prefer the freedom of driving their own cars.			
California has plans to build a bullet train with an estimated cost of $98.5 billion.			
Bullet trains travel a minimum of 155 mph (249 kph).			
Bullet trains use electricity.			

Writing

Directions: Should the United States construct bullet trains? Explain your opinion and why you feel the way you do. Use the table on page 146 to help you write your opinion paragraph.

Edit and Revise

A strong opinion paragraph includes:

- an introductory sentence stating your opinion
- strong supporting details
- a concluding sentence

Writing

Mathematics

Directions: Solve each problem.

1.

$4\,\overline{)\,64}$

2. 31 × 8 = ________

3. 10 × 18 = ________

4. Divide 56 by 7.

____

5. 88 × 11 = ________

6. 7 × 8 = 56 × ☐

7.
$$\begin{array}{r} 153 \\ \times \quad 2 \\ \hline \end{array}$$
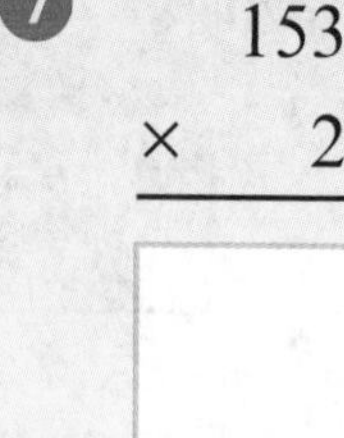

8. 37 × 24 = ________

9. 23 × 8 = ________

10. Divide 37 by 3.

____

11. 65 ÷ 10 = ________

12. Divide 82 by 4.

____

Directions: Solve each problem.

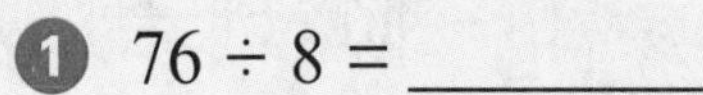

1. $76 \div 8 =$ ________

2. $\frac{1}{8}$ of 40 is ________

3. 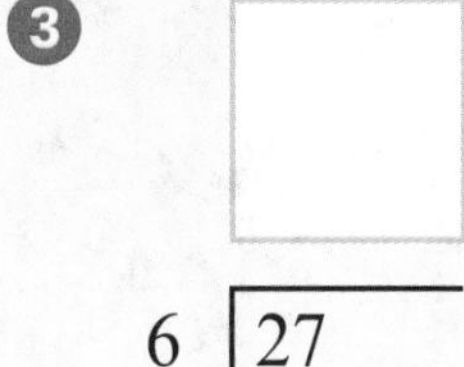

$6\overline{)27}$

4. Divide 4 into 90. ________

5. $\frac{1}{8}$ of 80 is ________

6. 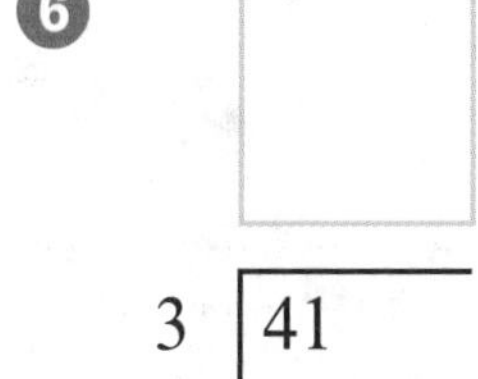

$3\overline{)41}$

7. $34 \times 28 =$ ________

8. $44 \div 5 =$ ________

9. 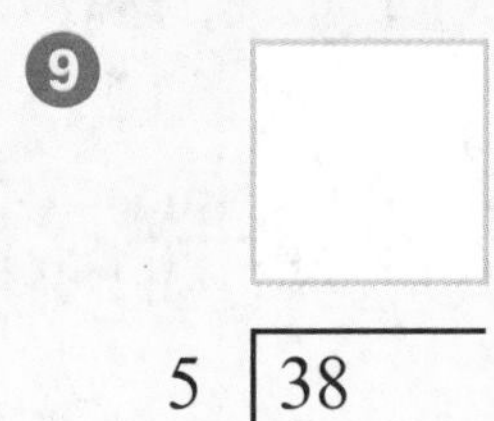

$5\overline{)38}$

10. Multiply 34 and 3. ________

11. $\frac{1}{8}$ of 120 is ________

12. 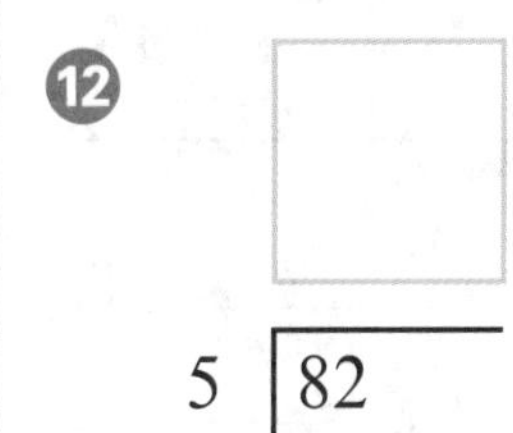

$5\overline{)82}$

Mathematics

Directions: Read and solve the problem.

Mr. Ly asks his students to write addition equations with a sum of $\frac{60}{100}$. He tells the class that one addend must have a denominator of 10 and the other addend must have a denominator of 100.

1. Write three equations. Show your work to prove your equations are correct.

$$\frac{\square}{10} + \frac{\square}{100} = \frac{60}{100}$$

$$\frac{\square}{10} + \frac{\square}{100} = \frac{60}{100}$$

$$\frac{\square}{10} + \frac{\square}{100} = \frac{60}{100}$$

2. Choose one of your equations. Write a story problem that represents the equation.

____

____

____

____

____

Problem Solving

Directions: Read and solve the problem.

Evan's teacher challenged the class to express 0.57 in as many ways as possible. Evan's group wrote their answers using a thinking web. If you were Evan's teacher, would you accept their responses as correct? Explain your reasoning.

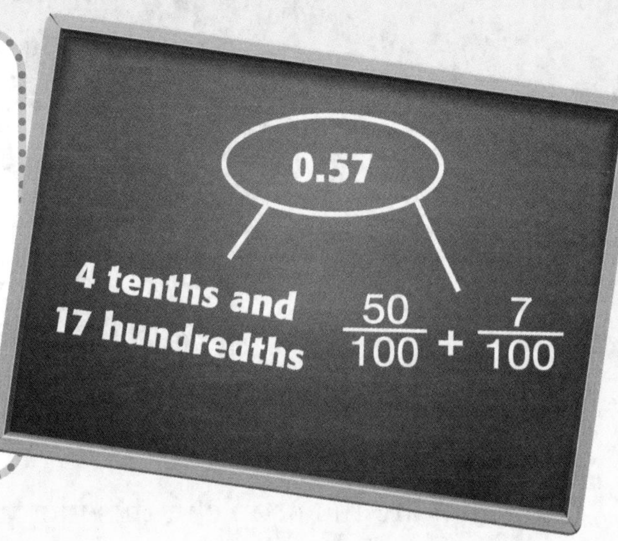

Problem Solving

1. What is "4 tenths and 17 hundredths" written in fraction form? What result will you get by combining these fractions? Should Evan's teacher accept this response from the group?

____

____

2. What is the sum of $\frac{50}{100}$ and $\frac{7}{100}$ in fraction form? What is the sum in decimal form? Should Evan's teacher accept this response from the group?

____

____

3. Contribute at least four more unique ways to express 0.57 on the thinking web.

Social Studies

Directions: Study the picture. Then, answer the questions.

1. What are the people in this picture doing?

2. How are they helping their community?

3. Why is it important to volunteer?

4. What are some ways you can volunteer at home or in your community?

Directions: Follow the steps in this experiment to discover what clean really means.

What You Need

- 3 plastic containers with lids
- 3 identical cloth samples
- 2 different detergent samples
- dirt
- warm water
- teaspoon

What to Do

1. Label three containers: Test 1, Test 2, and Test 3.
2. Rub a pinch of dirt into three of the cloth samples. Make sure each cloth is equally dirty.
3. Put one sample in each container. Half fill the containers with warm water.
4. Add 5 mL (1 tsp) of detergent to two containers. Use a different detergent in each. The last container should get no detergent.
5. Record which detergent went in which container.

   Test 1: ____________________

   Test 2: ____________________

   Test 3: ____________________
6. Shake each container for one minute. Remove and rinse the cloth samples. Make sure to keep track of which cloth was in which container. Describe the cloths:

   Test 1: ____________________

   Test 2: ____________________

   Test 3: ____________________
7. Which detergent cleaned the cloth the best?

   ____
8. Why do you think that happened?

   ____

   ____

   ____

Science

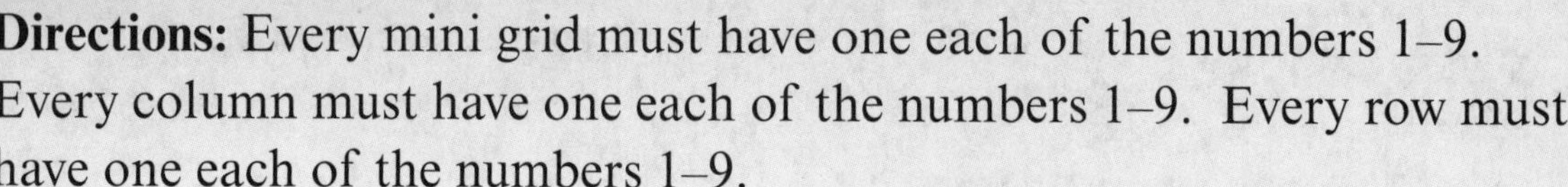

Directions: Every mini grid must have one each of the numbers 1–9. Every column must have one each of the numbers 1–9. Every row must have one each of the numbers 1–9.

		2	5		6			
4		8				6		7
	7		8		1		2	
9		3		8		1		4
			3		9			5
7		1		6	5	8		9
	3		1		8		4	
1		4	2			3		8
	8		6		4		1	

Directions: Play with a partner. Each player should place a small object at the start. Take turns rolling a number cube. Move your object to the number of spaces that you roll. Solve the problem in the space where you land. If you solve it correctly, stay on that space. If you solve it incorrectly, move back two spaces. Your partner can check your answer with a calculator. The first player to reach the finish line wins.

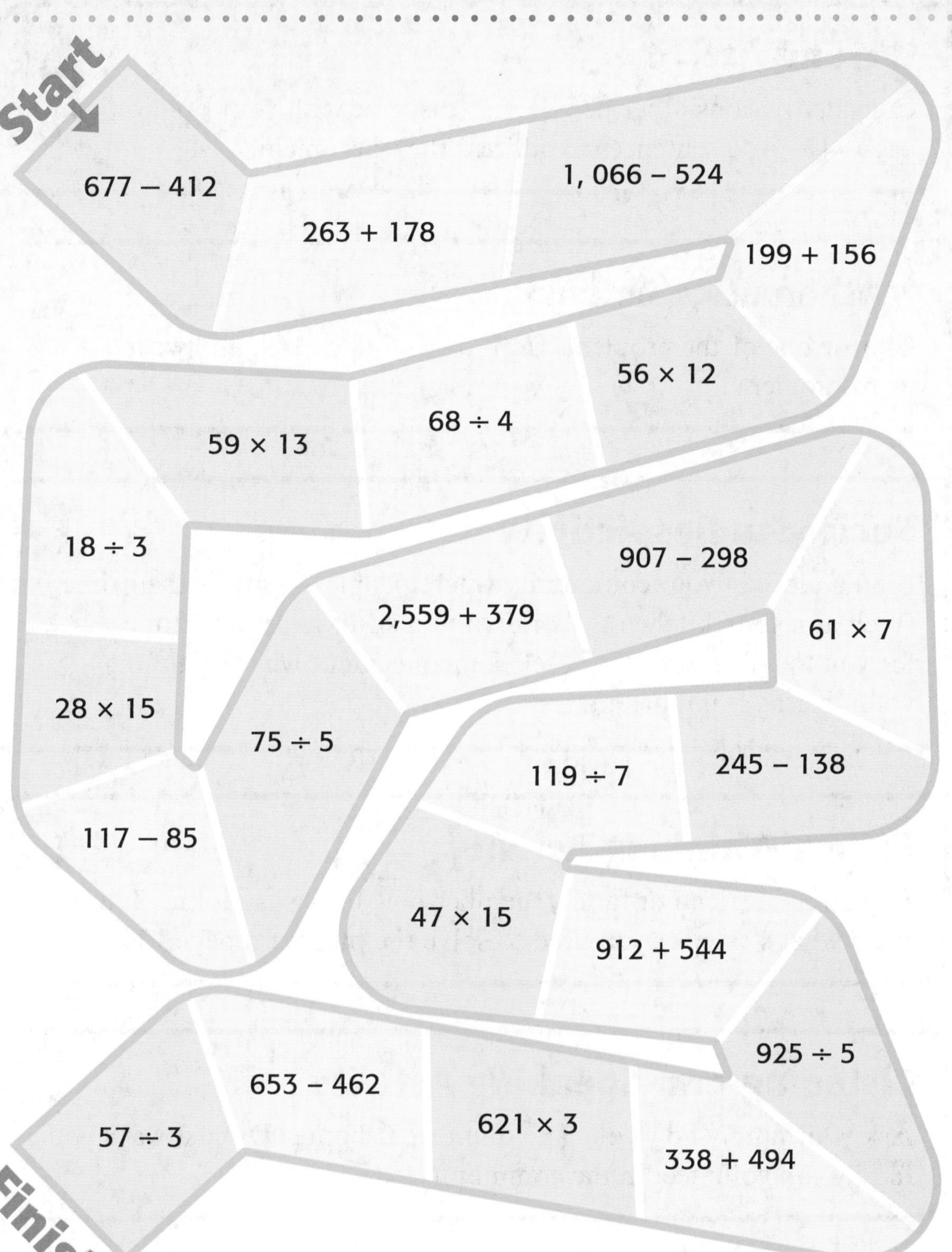

Spelling Activity

Review the contractions on page 144. Circle the letters that were replaced by the apostrophes.

Writing Activity

Consider reasons other people may disagree with your opinion on page 147. Add sentences to address their arguments.

Mathematics Activity

Choose one of the problems from pages 148 or 149, and write a word problem for it.

Social Studies Activity

Find a place in your community where people volunteer their time (such as a soup kitchen). Work with an adult to set up a time for you to volunteer. Then, tell someone about why you think volunteering is important.

Critical-Thinking Activity

Explain to a friend or family member how to play sudoku. Tell them what strategies you used to solve the puzzle on page 154.

Listening-and-Speaking Activity

Ask your family how you can volunteer at home. Discuss ways your family can volunteer in the community, too.

Answer Key

There are many open-ended pages, problems, and writing prompts in this book. For those activities, the answers will vary. Answers are only given in this answer key if they are specific.

page 7

1. B
2. D
3. B
4. A
5. C

page 8

1. B
2. D
3. A
4. B

page 9

1. Soft Sound: voice, bounce, germ, gentle, magic, gypsy
2. Hard Sound: complete, copy, country, guess

page 10

1. the, mars
2. boothill, graveyard, tombstone, arizona
3. the, boston, post, road
4. beijing, peking
5. can, mina
6. let's, main, street
7. lyla, ethan, sand, hill, river
8. cole, maybe
9. there, maine
10. john, mary

page 13

1. 29 kg
2. 26 stacks
3. 95¢
4. 375 beads
5. 4 liters
6. 3 times
7. $39.00
8. 8 and 9

page 14

1. 17
2. 8
3. 7
4. 2
5. 4
6. 7
7. 54
8. 7

page 15

1. There are six digits in standard form. The greatest place for this number is hundred thousands, followed by ten thousands, thousands, hundreds, tens, and ones.
2. 300,000; 60
3. Ten thousands and hundreds
4. Standard form: 305,061; Expanded form: 300,000 + 5,000 + 60 + 1.

page 16

1. Standard form: 210,101; Expanded form is 200,000 + 10,000 + 100 + 1. There are six digits in the number. The hundred thousands place is the greatest, and the value is 200,000. There is 1 ten thousand (10,000). There are 0 thousands. There is is 1 hundred (100). There are 0 tens and 1 one (1).
2. Expanded form: 700,000 + 9,000 + 200 + 5; Word form: seven hundred nine thousand, two hundred five. There are six digits in the number. The hundred thousands place is the greatest, and the value is 700,000. There are 0 ten thousands. There are 9 thousands (9,000). There are 2 hundreds (200). There are 0 tens and 5 ones (5).

page 19

A	C	D	F	B	E
E	F	B	D	C	A
B	A	E	C	F	D
C	D	F	A	E	B
F	B	A	E	D	C
D	E	C	B	A	F

page 22

1. D
2. C
3. A
4. A
5. C

page 23

1. C
2. A
3. D
4. D

page 24

1. /ow/: mound, hound, ground, surround, astound
2. /aw/: fought, brought, sought, thought, bought

page 25

1. Owen said, "I'm getting tired. I think it's time to go home."
2. "Shall we pick up a pizza for dinner tonight?" Riku's dad asked.
3. "What shall we do tomorrow?" Kala asked.
4. I would like to travel on a train, a ship, or a plane.
5. "Stop, thief!" cried the giant to Jack.
6. Amin likes to read books about writers.
7. A famous ocean liner sank on April 15, 1912.
8. The first snowboard was invented in Muskegon, Michigan.
9. I took Casey, the boy with the short hair, to dinner last night.
10. Heather left Los Angeles on February 2 of that year.

page 28

1. 3 cm
2. 10 kg
3. 50 mm
4. 200 mL
5. cubic units
6. 25 mm
7. 78 kg
8. 2 bottles
9. 100 cm

page 29

1. 4:01
2.  

3. 12:09
4. 
5. 7:26
6. 
7. 
8. 

page 30

1. There are 3,000 pieces of chocolate. The factory wants to put the chocolate into packages of 10.
2. Possible answer: I know that 10 tens is equal to 100. I also know that 100 tens is equal to 1,000.
3. 300 packages; explanations may include use of place value to determine the answer.

page 31

1. 40 boxes; divide to find how many groups of 100 are in 4,000; $4{,}000 \div 100 = 40$
2. 180 stacks; divide to find how many groups of 1,000 are in 180,000; $180{,}000 \div 1{,}000 = 180$

page 37

1. D
2. B
3. A
4. B
5. D

page 38

1. B
2. A
3. D
4. B

page 40

1. climb
2. fairy
3. seas
4. stare
5. would
6. sales
7. fell

page 43

1. 12 cm
2. 18 cm
3. 8 cm
4. 19 cm
5. 15 inches
6. 22 cm
7. 28 cm
8. 32 cm

page 44

1. 16 cm^2
2. 48 cm^2
3. 36 m^2
4. 81 cm^2
5. square feet
6. 8 m^2
7. 25 cm^2
8. 27 cm^2
9. 100 cm^2

page 45

606 kilometers; 2,500 – 1,894 = 606

page 46

1. Student 1 added the oranges instead of subtracting them. Student 2 subtracted each of the places incorrectly. Regrouping is required for the ones and hundreds places, and the student did not do this. The student simply subtracted the lesser digit from the greater digit and ignored the correct order.
2. The correct answer is 4,337 oranges. Strategies will vary but may include using a standard algorithm to subtract 8,186 – 3,849 = 4,337 or adding on to 3,849 on an open number line to find the total 8,186.

page 52

1. C
2. B
3. D
4. A
5. A

page 53

1. B
2. B
3. A
4. D
5. C

page 54

1. calves
2. leaves
3. loaves
4. knives
5. thieves
6. wives
7. lives
8. halves
9. shelves
10. wolves

page 55

1. Matteo, Jesse
2. cars
3. Springfield, Chicago
4. Judy Garland, *Meet Me in St. Louis*
5. ribbons, bikes
6. football
7. CBS, Los Angeles

page 58

1. D
2. $\frac{19}{100}$, 0.19
3. $\frac{1}{4}$
4. $\frac{3}{10}$
5. 6
6. $\frac{62}{100}$ or $\frac{31}{50}$
7. C

page 59

1. $\frac{25}{100}$ or $\frac{5}{20}$ or $\frac{1}{4}$
2. $\frac{40}{100}$ or $\frac{4}{10}$ or $\frac{2}{5}$
3. $\frac{4}{8}$
4. $\frac{8}{10}$
5. $\frac{81}{100}$
6. $\frac{7}{10}$
7. $\frac{2}{8}$ or $\frac{1}{4}$
8. $\frac{47}{100}$
9. $\frac{33}{100}$

page 60

1. Find all the ways to put 20 celery sticks into snack bags so that each snack bag has the same amount of celery sticks.
2. Listing factors of 20 will help find the possibilities for the number of snack bags the cafeteria manager can prepare.
3. 1 bag of 20 celery sticks; 2 bags of 10 celery sticks; 4 bags of 5 celery sticks; 5 bags of 4 celery sticks; 10 bags of 2 celery sticks; 20 bags of 1 celery stick

page 61

1 bag of 50 carrots; 2 bags of 25 carrots; 5 bags of 10 carrots; 10 bags of 5 carrots; 25 bags of 2 carrots; 50 bags of 1 carrot

page 64

A	D	E	M	O	C	R	A	C	Y	G	C
D	V	E	P	C	L	A	Q	E	Z	R	O
F	A	C	C	M	I	T	C	B	U	D	N
N	L	H	S	L	I	B	E	R	T	Y	S
V	U	K	V	Y	F	E	J	G	W	H	T
Y	E	W	J	K	R	D	S	V	L	M	I
S	S	X	T	O	E	F	A	U	E	T	T
R	M	C	L	P	E	Q	R	T	S	K	U
C	O	N	T	S	D	T	U	T	I	O	T
U	H	N	D	E	O	Y	F	P	U	O	I
B	N	X	W	X	M	G	M	O	Y	I	O
O	D	Z	A	G	N	P	E	R	I	A	N
I	N	D	E	P	E	N	D	E	N	C	E

page 67

1. D
2. A
3. B
4. D

page 68

1. C
2. B
3. D
4. D

page 69

1. widest
2. hottest
3. craziest
4. prettiest
5. funniest
6. tiniest
7. largest
8. nicest
9. calmest
10. happiest

page 70

1. tour
2. competed, won
3. celebrate
4. misses
5. named
6. can, ride
7. are, marry
8. lived
9. swam, walked
10. eats

page 71

three parts: nucleus, coma, tail
nucleus: solid center made of dust and ice
coma: gas and dust atmosphere around nucleus
two tails: dust and plasma
look like "dirty snowballs"

page 73

1. ten: 420; hundred: 400
2. ten: 870; hundred: 900
3. 130
4. 1,900
5. 500
6. 790
7. 400
8. ten: 4,830; hundred: 4,800; thousand: 5,000
9. 200
10. 1,300

page 74

1. 6 hours
2. 12
3. $48.00
4. 36 eggs
5. 21
6. 6 triangles should be colored yellow; 3 triangles should be colored blue.
7. 3 possible answers: Add 10 to get 50, 60; Multiply by 3, then 5 to get 120, 200; multiply by 3, then add 10 to get 120,130
8. 60 miles

page 75

Month	Expression Using Estimates	Estimated Texts Per Person
November	2,800 ÷ 4	700
December	800 ÷ 4	200

page 76

1. The multiplication problem should include 50 and 70 as factors and the product should equal 3,500. Possible answer: There are 70 passengers on each bus. There are 50 buses leaving the station every day. How many passengers are there altogether?
   $70 \times 50 = 3{,}500$.
   The division problem should include 3,500 as the dividend with the 50 and 70 as either the divisor or quotient. Possible answer: There are 3,500 apartment units in the city. Each apartment building has 70 units. How many apartment buildings are there in the city?
   $3{,}500 \div 70 = 50$.
2. Possible answer: The product is the number that represents the total. So, the greatest number is the product. In the division equation, I had to start with the product. The factors were the quotient and the divisor.

page 77

1. Brazil
2. Argentina
3. Colombia
4. C

page 79

3	2	5	4	6	1
6	4	1	3	5	2
2	1	6	5	4	3
4	5	3	2	1	6
1	3	4	6	2	5
5	6	2	1	3	4

page 83

1. A
2. C
3. C
4. A
5. B
6. C

page 84

1. supplies
2. blueberries
3. cavities
4. turkeys
5. chimneys
6. enemies
7. batteries
8. mysteries
9. pulleys
10. journeys

page 85

1. long, the
2. beautiful
3. the, black
4. decorative, the, best, the
5. a, huge
6. fast
7. blind
8. dust
9. the, very, slippery
10. the, fluffy, the, red

page 88

1. Cathy and Jose
2. 8 awards
3. Jahir: 23; Olivia: 15; Gerald: 35; Mimi: 3
4. $68

page 89

1. 180 inches
2. Allison
3. **Home Runs Hit**

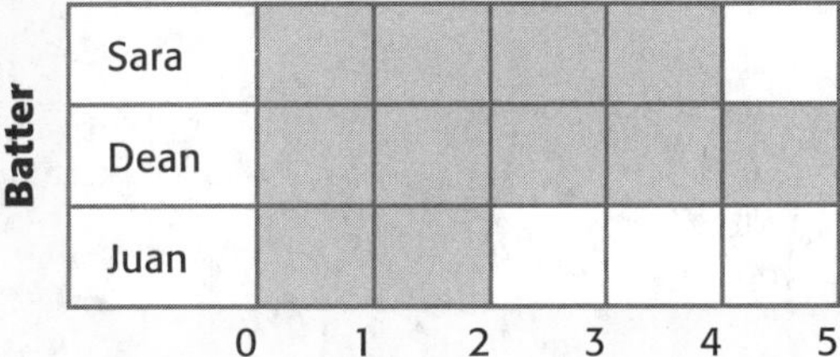

page 90

1. 54 books; $6 \times 9 = 54$
2. 42 books; $6 \times 7 = 42$
3. 102 books;
   $6 + (6 \times 9) + (6 \times 7) = 6 + 54 + 42 = 102$

page 91

1. 1×12; 2×6; 3×4
2. Possible answer: If I know the factor pairs of 12, I can use multiples of 10 to help me write multiplication equations with a product of 1,200.
3. Possible answer: I can multiply 1,200 by any factor, find the product, and write the division equation. For example, $1{,}200 \times 2 = 2{,}400$, so $2{,}400 \div 2$ must be 1,200.
4. Possible answers:
   $300 \times 4 = 1{,}200$; $30 \times 40 = 1{,}200$;
   $600 \times 2 = 1{,}200$; $60 \times 20 = 1{,}200$;
   $1{,}200 \times 1 = 1{,}200$;
   $9{,}600 \div 8 = 1{,}200$; $6{,}000 \div 5 = 1{,}200$;
   $4{,}800 \div 4 = 1{,}200$; $3{,}600 \div 3 = 1{,}200$;
   $2{,}400 \div 2 = 1{,}200$

page 98

1. B
2. D
3. D
4. C
5. C
6. C

page 99

1. slay; yals
2. stray; yarts
3. holiday; yadiloh
4. Monday; yadnoM
5. stain; niats
6. faith; htiaf
7. sprain; niarps
8. plain; nialp
9. aim; mia
10. afraid; diarfa

page 100

1. vary
2. pair
3. boulder
4. women
5. scene
6. writes
7. your

page 103

1. At least one line of symmetry should be drawn from vertex to opposite vertex or side to opposite side.
2. 5
3. At least one line of symmetry should be drawn from vertex to opposite vertex or side to opposite side.
4. At least one line of symmetry should be drawn from vertex to opposite vertex or side to opposite side.
5. rectangle
6. At least one line of symmetry should be drawn from any vertex to the opposite side.
7. hexagon

page 104

1. sphere
2. cylinder
3. 3; 3; 3
4. perpendicular
5. 4; 4; 2
6. parallelogram, rhombus, or trapezoid
7. A parallel line should be drawn, which does not cross the given line.

page 105

1. It must have at least 4 sides.
2. Shape should have two parallel lines and two right angles.
3. Any polygon that has one set of parallel sides and two right angles.

page 106

1. Sketch should include: sun, moon, moon, star, star, sun, moon, moon, star, star
2. This can help solve the problem because there are 10 beads in that pattern, and 10 × 10 is 100. The 100th bead must be a star.
3. Answers will vary. Check that the 100th bead is accurate based on the pattern created. Possible answer: In the pattern sun, star, moon, the 100th bead will be a sun because the pattern would start over with the 100th bead.

page 113

1. A
2. D
3. B
4. B
5. A
6. D

page 115

1. on a cone
2. on the wrong feet
3. at the shoulders
4. on the list
5. after nearly five years
6. in the rink
7. except for three white paws
8. in a show
9. down the street
10. In the basement

page 116

It was made with interchangeable parts, so the car took less time to make.
Workers were paid $5.00 a day; most other workers were paid $2.34 a day.
It was made on a moving assemby line, so the car was less expensive to make.
It was introduced in October 1908.
It was nicknamed the "Tin Lizzie."

page 118

1. 3,000 mL or 3 L
2. 700 grams
3. 31 m
4. $10
5. 264 times
6. $4.00
7. $50

page 119

1. yes
2. 15
3. no
4. 30
5. 0.73
6. 0.37
7. $\frac{35}{100}$ or $\frac{7}{20}$
8. $\frac{2}{10}$ or $\frac{1}{5}$
9. $\frac{45}{100}$ or $\frac{9}{20}$
10. 6

page 120

1. The number of lollipops in each group
2. The number of groups
3. Possible answers: $57 \div 9 = 6$ remainder 3; $57 \div 3 = 18$ remainder 3; $57 \div 6 = 9$ remainder 3; $57 \div 27 = 2$ remainder 3

page 121

1. 80 bottles; $20 \times 4 = 80$
2. 192 bottles; $64 \times 3 = 192$
3. 34 packages of water; $80 + 192 = 272$; $272 \div 8 = 34$; or $80 \div 8 = 10$; $192 \div 8 = 24$; $10 + 24 = 34$

page 128

1. C
2. A
3. D
4. C
5. C
6. C

page 130

1. the, a
2. the
3. the, the
4. the
5. a
6. The
7. The
8. A
9. a
10. the

page 133

1. 1, 2, 3, 6
2. 1, 2, 4
3. 1, 3, 9
4. 1, 2, 4, 8, 16
5. 1, 2, 3, 6, 9, 18
6. 1, 2, 4, 8
7. 1, 2, 3, 4, 6, 8, 12, 24
8. 1, 2, 4, 5, 10, 20
9. 1, 5, 25

page 134

1. 1, 2, 3, 4, 6, 9, 12, 18, 36
2. 1, 2, 3, 5, 6, 10, 15, 30
3. 8, 5, 7, 3
4. 8, 6, 8, 7
5. 6, 8, 10, 9
6. 7, 14, 21

page 135

1. Derrick practices soccer $\frac{1}{2}$ of the time. Derrick practices baseball $\frac{2}{7}$ of the time. Derrick has an off-day $\frac{3}{14}$ of the time.
2.

Sunday	Monday	Tuesday	Wednesday	Thursday	Friday	Saturday
B	X	X	X	B	X	X
X	B	X	X	X	B	X

Accept any fractions equivalent to $\frac{10}{14}$; Possible equivalent fractions: $\frac{5}{7} = \frac{15}{21} = \frac{20}{28}$

page 136

1.

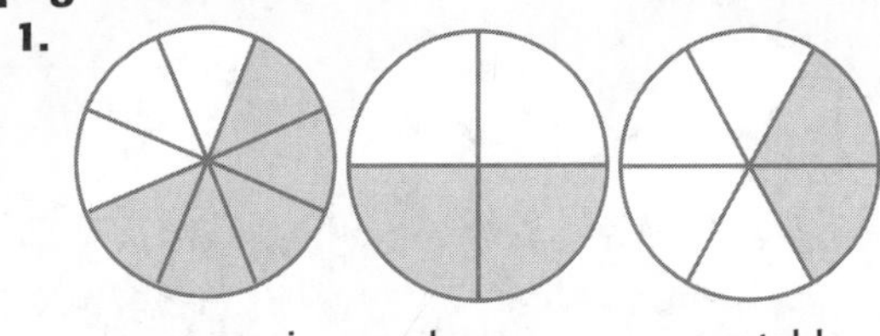

2. Pepperoni pizza: $\frac{3}{8}$ left over; cheese pizza; $\frac{2}{4}$ or $\frac{1}{2}$ left over; vegetable pizza: $\frac{4}{6}$ or $\frac{2}{3}$ left over
3. $\frac{3}{8}$, $\frac{2}{4}$, $\frac{4}{6}$; Possible strategies: fraction models; number lines; compare each fraction to $\frac{1}{2}$ as benchmark fraction; $\frac{3}{8}$ is less than $\frac{1}{2}$, $\frac{2}{4}$ is exactly $\frac{1}{2}$, and $\frac{4}{6}$ is greater than $\frac{1}{2}$.

page 143

1. A
2. D
3. B
4. D
5. D
6. C

page 144

1. you'd
2. they'll
3. would've
4. shouldn't
5. I'm
6. he'll
7. they'd
8. could've
9. I'd
10. we've

page 145

1. afford
2. except
3. busiest
4. probably
5. portion
6. foolish
7. dangerous
8. favorite
9. believe

page 148

1. 16
2. 248
3. 180
4. 8
5. 968
6. 1
7. 306
8. 888
9. 184
10. 12 R1
11. 6 R5
12. 20 R2

page 149

1. 9 R4
2. 5
3. 4 R3
4. 22 R2
5. 10
6. 13 R2
7. 952
8. 8 R4
9. 7 R3
10. 102
11. 15
12. 16 R2

page 150

1. Equations will vary, but the sum should equal $\frac{60}{100}$; Possible answers: $\frac{3}{10} + \frac{30}{100} = \frac{30}{100} + \frac{30}{100} = \frac{60}{100}$; $\frac{1}{10} + \frac{50}{100} = \frac{50}{100} + \frac{10}{100} = \frac{60}{100}$; $\frac{4}{10} + \frac{20}{100} = \frac{40}{100} + \frac{20}{100} = \frac{60}{100}$
2. Story problems will vary but should represent an equation written; Possible example: Shelby uses $\frac{50}{100}$ of a container of iced tea mix to make drinks for her guests. Then, she uses $\frac{1}{10}$ of that same container of mix to make the iced tea stronger. How much of the iced tea mix has Shelby used altogether?

page 151

1. $\frac{4}{10}$ and $\frac{17}{100}$; $\frac{57}{100}$; $\frac{4}{10} = \frac{40}{100}$; $\frac{40}{100} + \frac{17}{100} = \frac{57}{100}$; Yes, Evan's teacher should accept this response because $\frac{57}{100}$ is equal to 0.57.
2. $\frac{57}{100}$; 0.57; Yes, Evan's teacher should accept this response because $\frac{57}{100}$ is equal to 0.57.
3. Answers will vary but should include at least four more unique ways to express 0.57; Possible answers: 5 tenths and 7 hundredths; $\frac{57}{100}$; 57 hundredths; 2 tenths and 37 hundredths; $\frac{5}{10} + \frac{7}{100}$

page 154

3	9	2	5	7	6	4	8	1
4	1	8	9	2	3	6	5	7
6	7	5	8	4	1	9	2	3
9	5	3	7	8	2	1	6	4
8	4	6	3	1	9	2	7	5
7	2	1	4	6	5	8	3	9
2	3	7	1	9	8	5	4	6
1	6	4	2	5	7	3	9	8
5	8	9	6	3	4	7	1	2

Skills and Standards in This Book

Today's standards have created more consistency in how mathematics and English language arts are taught. In the past, states and school districts had their own standards for each grade level. However, what was taught at a specific grade in one location may have been taught at a different grade in another location. This made it difficult when students moved.

Today, many states and school districts have adopted new standards. This means that for the first time, there is greater consistency in what is being taught at each grade level, with the ultimate goal of getting students ready to be successful in college and in their careers.

Standards Features

The overall goal for the standards is to better prepare students for life. Today's standards have several key features:

- They describe what students should know and be able to do at each grade level.
- They are rigorous and dive deeply into the content.
- They require higher-level thinking and analysis.
- They require students to explain and justify answers.
- They are aimed at making sure students are prepared for college and/or their future careers.

Unit Outline

This book is designed to help your child meet today's rigorous standards. This section describes the standards-based skills covered in each unit of study.

Unit 1	• Read and answer questions about a narrative and a piece of nonfiction text. • Practice reading and writing spelling words. • Use correct capitalization. • Write an informative paragraph about Chihuahuas. • Use strategies to add, subtract, multiply, and divide.	• Write numbers in standard, expanded, and word form. • Identify people who make and enforce rules. • Observe the relationship between the angle of mirrors and the number of reflections.
Unit 2	• Read and answer questions about a narrative and a piece of nonfiction text. • Practice reading and writing spelling words. • Use correct punctuation. • Write a narrative about touring the Grand Canyon. • Estimate and measure liquid volume and lengths of objects.	• Tell time to the nearest minute. • Use strategies to multiply and divide large numbers. • Distinguish between power and authority. • Observe the relationship between vibration and sound.
Unit 3	• Read and answer questions about a narrative and a piece of nonfiction text. • Practice reading and writing spelling words. • Spell grade-appropriate words correctly. • Write an opinion paragraph about Beethoven's music.	• Calculate area and perimeter. • Fluently add, subtract, multiply, and divide. • Identify laws in the community. • Observe erosion.
Unit 4	• Read and answer questions about a narrative and a piece of nonfiction text. • Practice reading and writing spelling words. • Identify and use proper and common nouns. • Write a narrative about playing kickball.	• Express numbers as fractions and decimals. • List factors of numbers. • Analyze an excerpt from the Declaration of Independence. • Observe and measure wind.
Unit 5	• Read and answer questions about a narrative and a piece of nonfiction text. • Practice reading and writing spelling words. • Identify and use verbs. • Write an informative paragraph about comets.	• Round numbers to the nearest 10, 100, and 1,000. • Use strategies to solve word problems. • Analyze a map of South America. • Observe seeds sprouting.

Unit 6	• Read and answer questions about a narrative. • Practice reading and writing spelling words. • Identify adjectives. • Write a narrative about eating an ice cream cone.	• Use and interpret charts and graphs. • Use strategies to multiply and divide. • Identify goods and services. • Observe how fossils are made.
Unit 7	• Read and answer questions about a piece of nonfiction text. • Practice reading and writing spelling words. • Spell grade-appropriate words correctly. • Write an opinion paragraph about wind turbines.	• Identify lines of symmetry in polygons. • Identify attributes of polygons. • Make predictions using patterns. • Research westward expansion in the 1800s. • Observe acid-base reactions.
Unit 8	• Read and answer questions about a narrative. • Practice reading and writing spelling words. • Identify prepositional phrases. • Write an informative paragraph about the Model-T car.	• Use the four operations to solve word problems. • Express numbers as fractions and decimals. • Create a map of the local area. • Investigate how digestion works.
Unit 9	• Read and answer questions about a piece of nonfiction text. • Practice reading and writing spelling words. • Identify articles. • Write a narrative about going ice skating.	• List factors of numbers. • Use and interpret charts. • Compare fractions with different numerators and denominators. • Identify characteristics of a good leader. • Use a control to isolate variables.
Unit 10	• Read and answer questions about a narrative. • Practice reading and writing spelling words. • Spell grade-appropriate words correctly. • Write an opinion paragraph about bullet trains. • Multiply and divide multi-digit numbers.	• Identify and use equivalent fractions and decimals. • Add fractions with common denominators. • Identify ways to volunteer. • Create an experiment to test three different detergents.

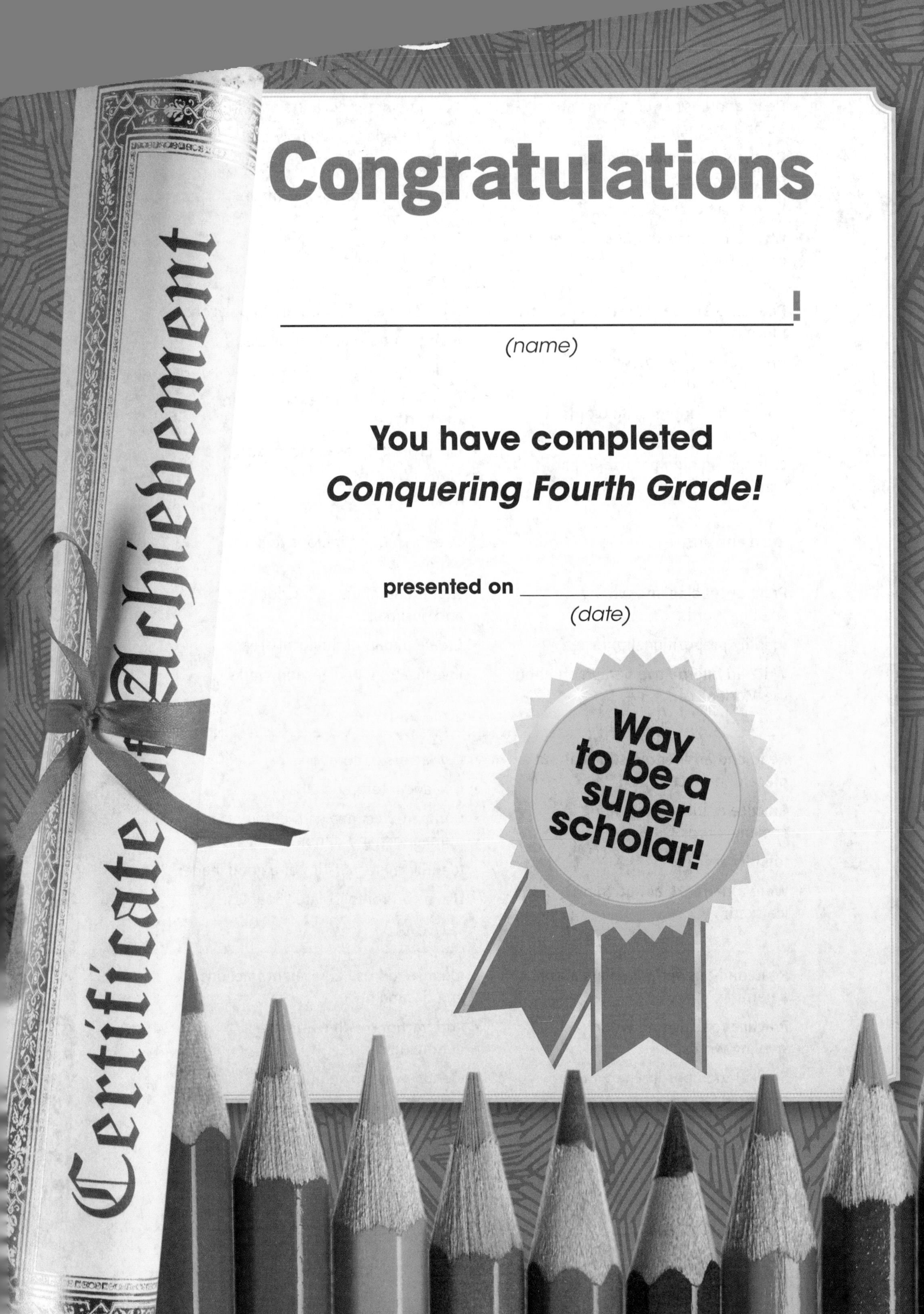
Congratulations
!
(name)
You have completed
Conquering Fourth Grade!
presented on
(date)
Way to be a super scholar!
Certificate of Achievement